D0093846

"*Experiencing Spiritual Breakthroughs* is a great book by a great man of God who has had an enormous impact on me, my family, and thousands of business and professional men around the country. Bruce Wilkinson is unsurpassed in focusing on biblical character lived out daily in bite-sized, practical, life-to-life truth."

PHIL DOWNER
PRESIDENT, CBMC MINISTRY TO THE MARKETPLACE

"If you or anyone you know desires to have God's light expose an area of struggle in your own life—and experience a true spiritual break-through—read this book! A must for every believer's library."

DR. RALEIGH B. WASHINGTON
VICE PRESIDENT OF RECONCILIATION, PROMISE KEEPERS

"*Experiencing Spiritual Breakthroughs* is hard hitting, direct, and honest as it deals with how Christians have their own private agendas. It discusses sin realistically, coupled with confession, cleansing, and restoration. This is Bruce at his best!"

JOHN E. KYLE
SENIOR VICE PRESIDENT, EVANGELICAL FELLOWSHIP OF MISSION AGENCIES

"Bruce Wilkinson has done it again. His profound understanding of God's Word, coupled with Spirit-led insight, creative metaphors, and practical guides to application, provide tremendous motivation and encouragement to all of us."

PAT MACMILLAN
TEAM RESOURCES, INC.

"Every page of this book penetrates the core and very center of our existence."

MARGARET A. BRIDGES
ADMINISTRATOR
TABERNACLE SCHOOL, CONCORD, CALIFORNIA

EXPERIENCING

SPIRITUAL

BREAKTHROUGHS

DR. BRUCE H. WILKINSON

Multnomah® Publishers *Sisters, Oregon*

EXPERIENCING SPIRITUAL BREAKTHROUGHS
published by Multnomah Publishers, Inc.

© 1999 by Bruce Wilkinson
International Standard Book Number: 1-57673-929-5

Cover design by The Office of Bill Chiaravalle
Cover illustration by Mike Wepplo

Unless otherwise indicated, Scripture quotations are from:
The Holy Bible, New King James Version
© 1982 by Thomas Nelson, Inc. Used by permission

Other Scripture quotations:
The Holy Bible, King James Version (KJV)

Multnomah is a trademark of Multnomah Publishers, Inc.,
and is registered in the U.S. Patent and Trademark Office.
The colophon is a trademark of Multnomah Publishers, Inc.

Printed in the United States of America

For information:
MULTNOMAH PUBLISHERS, INC.
POST OFFICE BOX 1720
SISTERS, OREGON 97759

LIBRARY OF CONGRESS CATALOGING-IN-PUBLICATION DATA
Wilkinson, Bruce.
    Experiencing spiritual breakthroughs / by Bruce Wilkinson.
        p. cm.   ISBN 1-57673-929-5 (alk. paper)
    1. Spirituality. 2. Spouses—Religious life. 3. Parents—Religious life. I. Title.
BV4501.2.W53255 1999   99-052434
248.4–dc21

02 03 04 05 — 9 8 7 6 5

TABLE OF CONTENTS

DEDICATION

For this book, I asked myself: "Who is the one person I know who sits in the First Chair as a way of life as well as enabling me the most to pursue that First Chair throughout my own pilgrimage?" The answer came immediately. One person has, for more than thirty years, been a model to me of holiness and passion for the Lord Jesus Christ. One person continues to be my greatest inspiration and encourager in my process of becoming more of a true disciple of Jesus Christ.

Without her love, prayers, and support, this book could never have been written because I couldn't have written it—I wouldn't have witnessed its truth in her life, or been able to pay the price to experience it in my own. So it gives me great pleasure to dedicate *Experiencing Spiritual Breakthroughs* to my fellow pilgrim, soulmate, spiritual warrior, closest friend, and wife…

Darlene M. Wilkinson

ACKNOWLEDGMENTS

I'm indebted to numerous individuals for their encouragement and support in the development of this book. First, to my good friend, John Van Diest—thank you for twenty years of friendship, exhortation, and stubborn prodding to get this material beyond sermons and tapes and into a book. Without you, this book would have stayed only a dream.

To Coach Bill McCartney of the Promise Keepers—thank you for your invitation and encouragement to preach this message to hundreds of thousands of men, and to call for their response.

To Gene Mims of LifeWay Resources who challenged me to revise the Three Chairs video series and materials—many thanks, my friend.

To Walk Thru the Bible's board and staff, who have been a source of such great strength and joy over many years—thank you! May this tool extend our ministry around the world together.

To Chip MacGregor who worked so diligently on this project in the earlier days, I extend my heartiest thanks. To Don Jacobson and the rest of the fine Multnomah team—it has been a pleasure to work with men and women so committed to the mission and the message.

To my editors, David and Heather Kopp—what a joy and privilege to share in the considerable gift God has placed in you! With rare skill, you have transformed these concepts to beauty on the page, greatly improving both their content and emotional impact. May you rejoice in this fruit of your ministry as it reaches around the world for Christ.

And lastly, to my family members, who have every right to be delighted that this project is finally done—thank you for your patience, understanding, encouragement, and love.

INTRODUCTION

So many Christians have shared with me their frustrations about making spiritual breakthroughs. "Seems like I've tried everything and nothing works," they say. "Maybe I'm expecting something that's possible for super saints, but not for me."

Friend, what you hope for is possible! In fact, God has been waiting for this moment. And he promises to meet you on your quest of a lifetime: "'And you will seek Me and find Me when you search for Me with all your heart. I will be found by you,' says the LORD" (Jeremiah 29:13–14).

I've written this book specifically for you—a believer who is ready to take action for lasting life change. *Experiencing Spiritual Breakthroughs* invites you to bring your most real, deeply felt needs for growth and change into a direct encounter with what God has to offer.

Besides this volume, several companion tools are available to help you. *Thirty Days to Experiencing Spiritual Breakthroughs* is a collection of daily readings from the finest Bible teachers and writers. Each reading addresses a key issue that we'll be discussing in the following pages. And be sure not to miss the resources listed on page 247 in the volume you're holding. These outstanding print, audio, and video resources from Walk Thru the Bible ministries can help make your learning experience, individually or in a group, much more satisfying and complete.

Regardless of where you are in your spiritual journey, exciting prospects lie just ahead. As roadblocks get pushed aside, obstacles overcome, and old, destructive habits left behind, you'll experience immediate and profound change. God's wonderful purposes will begin to unfold in and around you. By the time you put this book down, you're going to be a different person. Why? Because you'll have experienced the specific spiritual breakthroughs your loving Lord has always intended for you.

Blessings on the journey!

EXPERIENCING

SPIRITUAL

BREAKTHROUGHS

Experiencing Spiritual Breakthroughs

Chapter One

Moments of Destiny

THE TRUTH ABOUT SPIRITUAL BREAKTHROUGHS

*C*all it a breakthrough moment—one of those flashes of absolute clarity, perfect sense…perfect terror. *I'm not going to make it out of here alive!*

Of course, that's not what I said to my three climbing buddies. After all, this was a wilderness training program for executives—a week of taking things to extremes in search of industrial-strength bonding and confidence. Only tough hombres need apply.

"Guys," I said, as I squinted up into the sun, "what were we thinking?"

Above us loomed a hundred and fifty feet of sheer rock. Our objective was simple—get the three of us from down here to up there. A rope snaked down the cliff face to coil menacingly at our feet.

It didn't help that several teammates had already succeeded at this training phase and were now throwing down encouragements from on high. Or that my partner Al was busy breaking our crisis into bite sizes.

"One hundred and fifty feet is about fifteen stories, I figure," he said. "Maybe six seconds of free-fall time. Hit the ground right here with about as much force as, oh, maybe—"

"Al," I broke in, "why don't you hand the rope to Jeff." Fortunately for my quaking knees, Jeff had been tagged to go up next.

I helped him get clipped into the safety harness. The whole point of this trial-by-rock was to face down our fears. By learning to trust not only our equipment but also the other men on our team, we would break through to a higher level of personal confidence and team spirit.

"The man on the top is working with you every step of the way," our climbing coach had said. "The gear is top-rated. You'll do fine, especially if you don't look down."

When Jeff was securely in his harness, he yelled up, "I'm ready! Who's holding my line? My life is in your hands!"

"Vince!" came the reply from far above.

Suddenly Jeff froze, then stepped back and unclipped his harness. Clearly, he wasn't going up. He started waving his hands and shaking his head to the team above. "I'm not taking one step up this rock with that guy holding my rope!" he shouted. "Get me somebody else!"

In the shocked silence that followed, a feeling even more sickening than the fear of heights hit my stomach. It was imagining the utter embarrassment of Vince, the man on top, rejected as an untrustworthy climbing partner. It was the shattering awareness that all the camaraderie we'd been building piece by piece for days was about to fall apart.

The three of us looked up. The crew above peered down. And none of us knew what to do next.

Until Al stepped up. I heard a click. Al was buckling himself into the dangling harness. In a moment he was leaning into the rope.

"Vince!" he yelled.

"Yeah?"

"You ready?"

"I'm ready!" came back the reply.

"Here I come!" yelled Al. And he started up the face of the wall.

When Al was only about, oh, maybe one second of free-fall time up that cliff, I had my second breakthrough moment. My knees were still jelly, but at least I was breathing again. *You're going to be okay,* said that little voice. *You're going to climb that cliff just fine…all the way to the top.*

And by the end of the day, that's exactly what I had done.

REACHING FOR MORE

The book you're holding is about spiritual breakthroughs. It's about taking risky steps toward life-altering change—even when, especially when, you feel frozen in place, overwhelmed by obstacles.

Since you're reading this page, I imagine you're asking the Lord for a breakthrough in a vital area of your life. Maybe you have taken stock of what you've accomplished, who you have become, how your marriage is unfolding, or how your kids are turning out. As you have looked over that inventory scribbled down somewhere in your heart, you have been disappointed or even deeply dismayed.

I've seen the longing for personal and spiritual change written across thousands of faces.

Or maybe you simply realize it's time to step up to a new level of commitment in your walk with God. Getting stuck or sliding back isn't for you. You're a committed spiritual climber, anxious to press on toward maturity and a fuller experience of the Lord's best for your life.

Now here you are, looking up at that rock wall, squinting into the sun. *Lord, I'm here. I want to change. I want Your best. Help me up!*

In my thirty years of ministry, I've seen the longing for personal and spiritual change written across thousands of faces. I've preached to stadiums full of gung ho seekers and counseled one-on-one with dozens of earnest women and men. Their questions are surprisingly similar:

What am I missing?

What is God's abundant best for my life and my family—and can I experience it personally?

What will it cost?

How can I be sure I won't fail again this time?

Where do I start?

How can I pass this kind of vital Christian experience along to my children?

You've seen them—maybe you have been one of them, too: they attend church, go to special meetings, read the latest self-help book. They start to make a new commitment. Then the rock wall of change overwhelms them. "I'll never get up to the top anyway," they reason. They falter, slipping back to what feels comfortable.

And what happens then? Their spiritual life drifts. Their relationships bump along. Their kids wobble off course.

But the Christian life wasn't meant to turn out that way. In His Word, God has given us simple but powerful principles that enable us to experience meaningful and lasting breakthroughs in key areas of our lives.

This book will show you, perhaps for the first time, not only where God is inviting you to make a change in your life, but how to do it. Friend, I can say that with confidence because I've seen the results in thousand of people just like you. As God opens your eyes page by page, you're going to have more "aha!" moments than you ever thought possible!

THE GEOGRAPHY OF CHANGE

You've probably noticed that your life seems to move from a season of security and rest, into a season of disruption and insecurity, and back again. Your life is neither a steady growth line nor an endless plateau. To put it another way, you're traveling through the geography of change if you move forward across a flat plateau, content with where you are; you're faced with a bump or a cliff, a challenge or an obstacle; you falter and turn away, choosing instead to stay on your plateau, maybe even step back a safe distance from that cliff. Or you seize the opportunity for a breakthrough and begin to climb; you break out onto a summit where you consolidate your gains; you begin moving forward again, across another, higher plateau.

Notice the place in the geography of change where you, the spiritual climber, must make a crucial choice. Your hand is on the rope. Your eyes are looking up. Your pulse is rising—yes, you've got it—welcome to the bottom of the cliff!

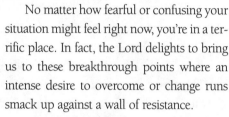

Breakthroughs have ultimately controlled nearly every area of my life.

No matter how fearful or confusing your situation might feel right now, you're in a terrific place. In fact, the Lord delights to bring us to these breakthrough points where an intense desire to overcome or change runs smack up against a wall of resistance.

As I think back to my rock-climbing experience, I see how much it changed all of us. We learned big lessons about trust and teamwork and taking risks. Some things will always be possible for us now that weren't before. By the time I had clambered to safety at the summit and given Vince a high-five, I had literally reached a new plateau of living.

Have you noticed how few turning points like that we experience in our lives? For most of us, I believe, fewer than a dozen. Yet we all measure our lives by them because we know without a doubt that they have made us what we are. I see clearly that breakthroughs have ultimately controlled nearly every area of my life. How thankful I am that at each step of the way, someone reached out to help me when I felt hopelessly alone, looking up at nothing but rock.

A ROPE HAS TWO ENDS

Do you know why Jeff stepped out of that climbing harness that day? I'll tell you. Something had happened between him and Vince in the past. Vince, the climber at the top, had broken his word to Jeff in a business deal. Let him down big-time. Jeff hadn't thought about it much lately, and it seemed to be a dead issue…until he stepped into that harness with his betrayer holding the line. At that moment, he suddenly had to trust Vince with his life, and he couldn't.

Oh, those painful moments while we waited to see what would happen. The whole time Al was working up the rock face, Jeff's challenge rang in our ears: *"Who's holding the line? My life is in your hands!"* Could Jeff break through to trust? And could Vince prove himself worthy of it?

I'm happy to say that both men made a breakthrough that day. After Al had scrambled safely to the summit, Vince leaned over the edge.

"Hey, Jeff?" A long pause. We all held our breath.

"Yeah," came the reply from the climber below.

"I'm just not that Vince anymore! I betrayed you in that business deal, and I'm sorry. I'll never do it again. Will you forgive me?" he yelled. "And I'm not giving this rope to anybody else. I'm asking you to trust me. My life is in your hands, too!" And he threw down the safety line.

You never have to get up that rock face of change alone. God is always at work on His end of the rope. You can reach for change with full confidence in the Person above you!

Jeff must have been doing some thinking, because this time he didn't hesitate. He snapped himself in, and—one step, one grasp, one pull of the rope—both men left the past behind.

I tell you this story because no one can move toward change without a significant level of trust in a good outcome. Past failures and hurts and present fears can hold you back. But friend, as a follower of Christ, you never have to balk at trusting God's good intentions for you or His power to accomplish them in your life.

Think of Christian growth as a rope with two ends—and a hundred and fifty feet of vertical rock face between them. On one end of the rope is you. As you grasp the possibilities and strain toward maturity with all your might, you'll fear failure, discomfort, opposition, the unknown. Your head will spin. Your knees will quake. But here's the great news: You never have to get up that rock face of change alone. God is always at work on His end of the rope. You can reach for change with full confidence in the Person above you!

In fact, a tremendous power is already flowing through your life.

Here's what I mean: one of the most important things we can say about any genuine spiritual breakthrough is that it is also God's work. "I thank my God every time I remember you," Paul wrote to the Philippian believers, "Being confident of this, that *he who began a good work in you will carry it on to completion* until the day of Christ Jesus" (Philippians 1:3, 6, emphasis added).

This is the part of personal change that never appears in most teaching. "Spirituality" has never been more popular, even in secular circles. But it seems to be taken up less and less with God and what He has said, and more and more with human-centered techniques. But these approaches gloss over a big problem—*the spiritual climber is trying to make a breakthrough alone.*

Christians know otherwise! It is the Lord Himself who is wooing us toward a spiritual breakthrough. Later in the same letter to the Philippians, Paul urges, "Therefore, my dear friends…continue to work out your salvation with fear and trembling, for it is God who works in you to will and to act according to his good purpose" (2:12–13).

It is the Lord Himself who will hold us fast, empower us, and encourage us on as we climb. And we can trust Him with our lives.

DID YOU SAY CHAIRS?

Every once in a while, an idea comes along which seems to grip people, and the illustration of the Three Chairs is one. In the next chapter I will introduce you to a conceptual model I'll be referring to throughout this book called the principle of the Three Chairs. I've watched as God has used the truths conveyed here to help thousands around the world respond to His loving tug, choose a new course, and experience meaningful, lasting change.

Each of the Three Chairs represent a different type of person and faith, three different levels of commitment toward God. If you are a Christian, then you have sat in every one of them at one time of your life or another. It won't take long for you to discover which of these Chairs you occupy and how they relate to nearly everything in your life. You will also discover incredible insights about your life, unlocking reasons you think and act the way that you do. You'll understand your parents and their influence on you in a different way than ever before. And as you reflect on the Chair that you sit in, you may be shocked at how dramatically your Chair of choice influences the spiritual lives of your children and grandchildren.

My goal is to help you recognize which Chair you and your family sit in and then to help you make the breakthroughs necessary to move you and those you love into the Chair where you really want to be—and help you stay there.

Throughout this book, we'll spend time examining how these Chairs relate to three key areas of life—actually, the three key relationships you have in life—and how we can make spiritual (God-motivated and God-helped) breakthroughs in each:

- your marriage
- your family
- your relationship with the Lord

In each chapter, we'll focus on a specific area, determine where you may need a dramatic change, and help you respond to God's invitation to personal growth, maturity, and blessing.

THE VIEW FROM THE SUMMIT

Recently I spent time with the CEO of a major, national corporation. On the outside, his life couldn't have looked more successful or in order. But inside he was stuck at the bottom of the cliff, wrestling with God over a critical breakthrough issue in his life. We talked, prayed, and cried together, and by the time our conversation was over, he was a different man. As he was leaving, he said to me, "Bruce, I'll never forget this moment, because I know I'll never be the same man again."

That's a breakthrough. Looking back, you see one life. Looking ahead, you see another. Everything is different, changed, better.

Remember, friend, as God's dearly loved children, we never have to settle for being stranded at the bottom of the cliff. Our Father created us for a life of freedom, fulfillment, and service for His glory. With God's help, you're setting out to accomplish something good and important and full of promise.

It's time to reach for the rope.

Chapter Two

The Secret of the Three Chairs

WHERE DO YOU AND YOUR FAMILY SIT?

nce as I was walking across the grounds of a large conference center, the director approached me. He thanked me warmly for my presentations—I was speaking on the materials in this book. The response from those in attendance had been astounding, we both agreed. Then he said something I'll never forget.

"Dr. Wilkinson, I've been part of this conference ministry for some time, as you know. We only have good speakers here. I've noticed that what they have to say falls into three categories. Some come to inspire. Some to teach. What you do falls in the third category. You come to bring life change.

"These people—" the director paused to wave toward clusters of people around the conference grounds—"when they go home, they'll be different."

I can assure you he wasn't referring to some earthshaking platform talent on my part. Lasting life-change is simply what happens when we are confronted with God's truth and choose to respond. We're never the same again. Either we make a breakthrough and go forward, or we fall back. There's no neutral ground.

After you encounter the truths of the Chairs in this chapter, you won't be the same either. You will have a new and clear awareness of where you are spiritually—and that awareness will call for a decision on your part.

How do I know a simple picture can deliver such a weighty spiritual payload? Because I've seen it work in hundreds of thousands of lives. Let me be even more specific:

- The visual model of Three Chairs will help you understand where your life choices have taken you so far in your key values and relationships.
- The Chairs will set out for you in startling clarity God's best for you.
- They'll help you see where your past and present choices will probably take you and your family in the future.
- And knowing what Chair you occupy will help you know what to do next if you want spiritual growth.

This chapter is probably the most important one in the book—and may be the most challenging. But every potential breakthrough to follow will build on the principles laid out here. I pray that the Holy Spirit will open your heart and understanding to each truth.

THREE CHAIRS OF FAITH

In your mind's eye, picture three chairs on a well-lit stage. Each one represents a person's spiritual status before God. The chair on the left we'll call the First Chair; the chair in the middle, the Second Chair; and the chair on the right, the Third Chair. Taken together, I call them the Chairs of faith, because they provide an accurate picture of how every person on the planet is responding to God.

A First Chair believer is not only saved, but has gone beyond accepting the gift of salvation to willfully being under Christ's authority and direction. This person knows the Lord as a personal friend and Savior, and is developing a meaningful and growing relationship with Him for himself and those he's responsible for. The apostle Paul calls this the spiri-tual state.

In your mind, embroider the word *commitment* into the well-worn fabric of the First Chair.

Some people imagine they are First Chair Christians because they surge up to the First Chair briefly on the wave of a mountaintop experience or a deeply felt crisis that sparks an outpouring of gratitude and good intentions. But when the tide of powerful events and feelings recedes, their true status is revealed. These experiences are meaningful, to be sure, but First Chair living is anchored in a person's whole intellect, will, and heart.

The First Chair person is taken up in a lifelong journey toward spiritual maturity. Because obedience and singleness of purpose mark this condition, God's Spirit can lead a First Chair dweller upward to the kind of blessing, fulfillment, and personal effectiveness that God intends for all his children.

The Second Chair represents someone who has received new life in Christ but hasn't decided how little or much they will follow Him. He claims to believe all the same truths as someone in the First Chair, follows the Christian "lifestyle" in many outward ways, and usually has the best of intentions.

> *First Chair living is anchored in a person's whole intellect, will, and heart.*
>
>

But instability and inconsistency mark his course. Unless there's a spiritual wave rolling through his life, a Second Chair person quickly runs short on internal strength because certain bedrock commitments are missing. In time, Second Chair people tend to slide farther away from their First Chair kin and closer to their Third Chair neighbors. Eventually, their lifestyles for an extended time period may even become completely indistinguishable from the person who does not know Christ as Savior. Paul calls this the carnal state.

Embroider the word *compromise* across this chair.

This brings us to a critical truth that always hides under the word *compromise.* Lurking there, like a troll under the bridge, is simply another, competing commitment. That's why even though I use the word *commitment* to describe Chair One, I could easily use the same word to describe Chair Two.

Because underlying compromise is a deeply felt commitment to self. The Second Chair person has God on the tip of his tongue but self on the throne of his heart. Unless that root commitment changes, attempts at spiritual breakthrough won't bring lasting effects.

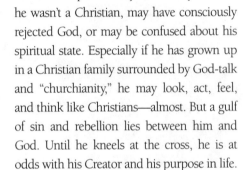

But the good news is that anyone with this status is a candidate for the most important spiritual breakthrough of all.

The Third Chair stands for someone who has not responded personally to God. A Third Chair person may have always known he wasn't a Christian, may have consciously rejected God, or may be confused about his spiritual state. Especially if he has grown up in a Christian family surrounded by God-talk and "churchianity," he may look, act, feel, and think like Christians—almost. But a gulf of sin and rebellion lies between him and God. Until he kneels at the cross, he is at odds with his Creator and his purpose in life.

Embroider the word *conflict* on this chair.

In some ways, the person in Chair Three may have a simpler life than either of the first two Chairs. He may have decided to live as if God doesn't exist. There's no higher authority to answer to, and no competing influence to tug him one way or the other. His decisions are based without apology on what he wants, period.

Since the person in the Third Chair has never received Christ as Savior, further attempts at spiritual breakthroughs will meet with frustrating defeat. He is still in what Paul called the natural state (see 1 Corinthians 2–3). He hasn't been spiritually reborn yet, and the work of God's Spirit must therefore be limited in his life.

But the good news is that anyone with this status is a candidate for the most important spiritual breakthrough of all. By responding in faith to Jesus Christ and asking for the forgiveness and new life He offers, Third Chair dwellers can step into the family of God today.

There you have it: three portraits, three spiritual states—and no exceptions. Every one of us fits into one of these descriptions, and perhaps like me, you know each Chair from personal experience.

Here's a summary of what we've seen so far:

A Snapshot of Everyone's Spiritual State		
Chair One	Chair Two	Chair Three
Commitment	Compromise	Conflict
Saved	Saved	Unsaved
Spiritual	Carnal	Natural

Now that I've described each Chair, it's time to see them in action in real life—as told in the Bible. My first encounter with these spiritual states I call the Three Chairs surfaced in the Old Testament. There in the space of a few chapters—from the end of Joshua to the beginning of Judges—I stumbled onto a dramatic presentation of the three states in close proximity, in the same span of time, and one generation after another.

Let me show you what I discovered.

THE GENERAL'S STORY

During his long lifetime, Joshua had risen from slave in Egypt, to servant of Moses, to desert spy, and finally to general and national leader during the conquest of Canaan. In Joshua 23 and 24, Joshua realizes that he is approaching the end of his life. By this time, the historic invasion of the Promised Land is complete. Israel is ready to enjoy the fruits of victory.

The craggy old general calls the nation's leaders together for a series of family meetings. "You yourselves have seen everything the Lord your God has done!" he tells them. "One of you routs a thousand because the Lord is with you!" (23:3, 10).

After Joshua reviews the entire saga of God's goodness to Israel, he throws down the challenge of a lifetime: "Choose for yourselves this day whom you will serve. But as for me and my household, we will serve the Lord" (24:15).

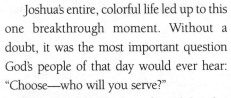

Without a doubt, it was the most important question God's people of that day would ever hear.

Joshua's entire, colorful life led up to this one breakthrough moment. Without a doubt, it was the most important question God's people of that day would ever hear: "Choose—who will you serve?"

The assembled leaders of Israel that day responded to Joshua without hesitation. They said yes—twice—and vowed at any cost to follow Joshua's example.

The years that followed proved them to be men of their word. The leaders, or elders as the Bible calls them, didn't turn aside to other gods. "Israel served the LORD all the days of Joshua, and all the days of the elders who outlived Joshua, who had known all the works of the LORD which He had done for Israel" (Joshua 24:31).

So far, so good. Yet as you trace the record of these elders, you find plenty of evidence that the elders served the Lord only partly, mostly when they found it to their advantage. For example, the only military action Israel had left to do after Joshua's death was to clean out the remaining pockets of resistance and pagan worship. But watch what happened instead:

"But Manasseh did not drive out the inhabitants of Beth Shean...
Nor did Ephraim drive out the Canaanites who dwelt in Gezer...
Neither did Zebulun drive out the inhabitants of Kitron..."
(Judges 1:27–30)

While Joshua had been fully committed to obeying God, the elders
were only partly committed. When the enemy tribes proved difficult to
remove, the elders decided to call off the battle and put the Canaanites
under tribute. No doubt this seemed like a terrific plan: no more fighting,
no more death, and plenty of money rolling in. Soon the Israelites and
their pagan neighbors were on good terms, and soon after that, both sides
began giving their sons and daughters in intermarriage agreements.

But what seemed like a new and stable portrait of God's people—living in
sensible compromise—shifted again. The next group of Israelites, known as
the children of the elders, were neither committed nor even compromised.

Read for yourself what happened:

"Another generation arose after them who did not know the
LORD...then the children of Israel did evil in the sight of the
LORD...and they forsook the LORD God of their fathers...and followed other gods...and provoked the LORD to anger...and behaved
more corruptly than their fathers...they did not cease from their
own doings nor from their stubborn way." (Judges 2:10–12, 19)

Here we have an unflattering description of people who lived in conflict with God. Perhaps they still told stories from their great-grandparents
about a miracle at the Red Sea. Maybe they remembered hearing from
their grandparents about Joshua's shout—"Choose!" But what they had
grown up with were parents who lived in peace and plenty. And what had
shaped their understanding of God was compromise.

How did this third group live? As God's people in name only. Today, we would say that they were nonbelievers—people who lived in a spiritual state apart from, and in conflict with, God.

Now we can show how Joshua's family sat in each of the Three Chairs. As we go along, we'll learn more about how and why they ended up where they did.

A SNAPSHOT OF THREE GENERATIONS		
JOSHUA	ELDERS	CHILDREN OF ELDERS
Chair One Commitment	Chair Two Compromise	Chair Three Conflict

It doesn't take a genius to look at the brief profiles of these three groups and see where spiritual breakthroughs are most needed. But our visual model of the Chairs has much more help to offer. For example:

- If a Chair or a generation equals a spiritual state, what would a person's life look like, and how would it be different, in each Chair?
- What would be the key spiritual breakthrough issues for each?
- What would be the long-term consequences of choosing a life in each Chair?

To answer those questions, I want to turn from Bible times and show how the truths of the Chairs are lived out today. We're going to look at how our seat of commitment affects three key areas—how we relate to God, how we relate to the world and choose our values, and how we relate to our families.

And to make it easier for you, I want to give each Chair a face and a name:

- In Chair One you'll find Julia, 35, a single mother of two who lives in New Jersey.
- Sitting in Chair Two, meet Ernie, 48. He works for a Christian radio station in Phoenix. He and his wife have three teenagers.
- And occupying Chair Three, meet Kate, 27, a software programmer in Minneapolis whose greatest passion at the moment is helping out at an inner-city soup kitchen on Saturdays.

As I describe the habits and views of these three, I predict that you are going to feel a growing kinship with one of them. Their thoughts will sound like yours, their dreams and priorities and problems like yours. In fact, by the end of this chapter, you'll have no doubt which of these Chairs has your name on it.

HOW THE CHAIRS RELATE TO GOD

God and Chair One. Julia thinks of God as a close and loving Father. This truth matters a lot to her because her own father was mostly distant and cool, and because as a single mom, she finds comfort in God's steadfast care.

She's as quick to talk about her relationship with the Lord as she might have been to talk about her marriage in the past ("I need time with Him," she might say, or "He's been talking to me about…" or "My spiritual relationship is really in a slump lately.") In fact, she talks—and listens—to God often during the day, whether it's in formal prayer or just while her car is stuck in traffic. If you asked her to draw a picture of this relationship, she would show two people sitting on her back porch watching her kids play. The two are deep in conversation. "That's me on the left with the cup of coffee," she'd say. "And that's Jesus on the right."

Her friends sometimes call her religious, but Julia never thinks of herself in that way. Religion has to do with rituals, dos and don'ts, and sacred buildings, she says. What she has is an intimate relationship that is both the source of and a result of her spiritual life, and that makes further spiri-tual maturity an inviting prospect.

"That's me on the left with the cup of coffee," she'd say. "And that's Jesus on the right."

Obedience isn't a word she uses much, but it's an unspoken assumption in how she relates to God. One of her favorite questions is, "God, what do You have for me to do today?" Obeying rarely seems burdensome when you're committed to a God you also love. Not that Julia is a robot—she has a lively imagination and quite a few artistic interests. But God comes before and over self as the one in charge.

God and Chair Two. Ernie knows more about God, the Bible, and what's going on in the Christian world than anybody in his group at church. He can debate the various positions on the end times right along with the best of them.

Ernie has been praying in public and private since he accepted Jesus as his Savior in junior high. But Ernie thinks of God more in terms of a powerful leader in a pretty messed-up world. Actually, it's occurred to Ernie that a person should keep enough distance between himself and God so that he can hear God's voice okay but interpret His wishes one way or another. Of course, he's very thankful for Christ's life, death, res-urrection, and promise of eternal life. And he knows a lot *about* Jesus. But if he were completely honest, he would probably choose the word "acquaintance" rather than relationship to describe the level of his friend-ship with Jesus.

When he prays, Ernie sometimes imagines himself as an unimportant person standing in a great throne room: he's hoping the king can hear him, but there's quite a bit of distance, a big crowd of more important people, and a lot of echoes, so he's not sure. He tends to pray the same things over and over again. Generally, he wants God's power to help him succeed, keep him and his family safe, multiply his investments, and "bless this food to our bodies, Amen."

Being a Christian is important to Ernie ("It's the right thing to do," he likes to say, adding with a grin, "as long as you don't overdo it!"). Anyway, Christian families turn out better, and church people on the whole are nicer to be around. Staying plugged in at church is a serious responsibility (Ernie hates to feel guilty). Since he works in Christian radio, his contacts at church help him get advertising support for his afternoon talk show.

"Obedience"? That's a '50s church word, he thinks; something his parents would have mumbled on about. Ernie thinks it's overrated—a code word the pastor brings out that means, "Give more money," or "Be a missionary in Zamboanga." Ernie prefers a term like "spiritual sensitivity." He believes God gave us our inner desires for a reason and we should follow them unless they collide with the Ten Commandments. If he had to choose, he'd put self first, God second. Don't misunderstand—Ernie really does care about what God wants. But what he usually *does* is what he wants.

God and Chair Three. Kate has forgotten most of what she learned from her grandmother when she was young, but she has strong feelings about the idea of God, and sometimes feels close to "Mother Earth" when she's camping in the Ozarks. The search for the historical Jesus has picqued her interest lately, as have the writings of the Dalai Lama and Stephen Jay Gould. But helping out at the soup kitchen really gives her a sense of significance.

To draw her proximity to God, Kate might show a microorganism submerged in an ocean of microorganisms. The few times when she has felt an inner conviction that God might want more from and for her, she has pulled back. Just the awareness that "God is everywhere and in everything" can bring her comfort—and that's enough. God is like gravity—a force that keeps you from floating away, but nothing you have to think about, right?

She dreams of a beautiful church wedding some day, but religion generally, and Christianity in particular, strike her as out-of-date institutions that oppress people around the world. She thinks televangelists are hucksters and "a personal relationship with Jesus Christ" is a slogan they use to raise money.

As a hard-driving, bright professional, Kate makes her decisions based on what makes the most sense for her career. She has tried meditation and psychotherapy to get in touch with her inner being. For her highest authority, she would point, not to God, but to her own enlightened self. She believes that the more she understands and follows her true self, the more she will be able to fulfill her destiny.

Here's how our portrait of the Chairs stacks up so far:

HOW THE CHAIRS RELATE TO GOD			
	FIRST CHAIR	SECOND CHAIR	THIRD CHAIR
Characteristic	Commitment	Compromise	Conflict
Illustration	Julia	Ernie	Kate
Knows God:	A close friend	Acquaintance	Awareness
Relates To God:	Relationship	Responsibility	Religion
Serves God:	God first, self second	Self first, God second	Self only

HOW THE CHAIRS RELATE TO THE WORLD

The World and Chair One. Julia loves life but she often feels at odds with the world around her. She'd rather trust the Bible for influence and direction as she makes decisions for herself or her two young children. Why? She has a nearly unshakable confidence in God's wisdom to know what's best for her, His goodness to desire it for her, and His strength to make it happen. Since the day ten years ago when she broke through to trusting God completely with her hopes and dreams, all the other tough choices that come along seem to fall into place with less struggle.

Julia's values—for example, on family priorities, what movies to watch, how to dress, how to relate to members of the opposite sex, the importance of saving and giving money—all these she bases on a careful examination of God's Word. Sometimes God's rules for living seem unpopular, difficult, and even painful, but her experience of testing these principles by living them out has given her a treasury of settled convictions. The main one is that God is entirely to be trusted. Because God's commands are so important in her life, Julia enjoys spending time regularly studying the Bible and listening for God's will for her and her family.

She sees her job portfolio at this stage in her family as making a home for her children and raising them to love and serve God. "Raising kids is my vocation—God's best for me right now," she says. To get by on her modest child support payments, she lives in a small house owned by her parents and takes in piecework on the side. When the children are more independent, she expects to update her education and work outside the home.

Either way, she has a strong sense that God, not any job, is her provider. Julia alarmed her unsaved father one day when she said, "My job is to obey God's calling, even if that means doing some things that are very difficult at times." She gets a lot of fulfillment from knowing that any job is simply another means for God to work through her to touch others.

The World and Chair Two. At first glance, Ernie and Julia seem to share a lot of the same concerns about worldly influence on their lifestyle choices. He's familiar with biblical teachings on most of the key points of morality and values, but unlike Julia, he interprets the Bible as a social document that best fit the times for which it was written. "These days if you want to know how to live like a Christian," he tells his friends, "you have to read the Bible with your 'commonsense spectacles' on."

Most of Ernie's beliefs about what's important in life have come down to him from his parents. Maybe it's because of his position at the radio station, but he seems to base most of his lifestyle choices on the going trends in Phoenix's booming Christian community. "Not being a stumbling block" is an important rule of thumb for Ernie. Actually, he's noticed a lot more latitude in Christian values lately as a higher percentage of new believers and marginally committed Christians make up his radio audience. This seems like progress to him because now it's not so embarrassing to be known as a Christian. He's noticed that some kinds of movies that used to highly offend him he now watches with his wife and teenagers. Good thing the kids are still pretty regular at the church youth group.

> *Most of
> Ernie's beliefs about
> what's important in life
> have come down to him
> from his parents.*

Ernie loves his work and says often that he thinks this is where God wants him. But a calling? That's something for missionaries. His prayers for God to bring him professional success seem to be working. Along with commissions on sales and some broadcasting work on the side, his work helps him provide well for his family.

The World and Chair Three. At odds with the world? Kate isn't sure what to make of the question. *Should a fish be at odds with the water it swims in?* she wonders. True, sometimes the world seems like a mean or dangerous place to Kate, but social change and the new possibilities it brings excite her. She loves to live on the cutting edge. To make a decision that she feels comfortable with, she simply measures what she wants with what society offers—and strikes the best deal possible.

Kate is articulate on current issues of concern. Her opinions—no on most abortions, yes on homosexual marriages, maybe on physician assisted suicide—are ones that make sense to her, period. Since truth and morality are mostly relative, Kate believes that what's really at stake is her right to think for herself.

For her, a person's job is the playing field for proving whether they're a winner or a loser in money, ambition, status, and personal fulfillment. In other words, what you're worth as a person. It's also a pretty good place to meet someone of the opposite sex with similar interests. Kate intends to win on all counts.

Here's the new information we've added about our three friends:

HOW THE CHAIRS RELATE TO THE WORLD		
	FIRST CHAIR	SECOND CHAIR	THIRD CHAIR
Characteristic	Commitment	Compromise	Conflict
Illustration	Julia	Ernie	Kate
Shaped by:	Scriptures	other Christians	society
Lives by:	convictions	beliefs	opinions
Sees work as:	God's calling	a job blessed by God	a proving ground

HOW THE CHAIRS RELATE TO MARRIAGE AND FAMILY

Marriage, Family, and Chair One. When Julia's husband walked out on their marriage, her confidence in herself, her faith, and her parenting prospects were badly shaken. But she pulled through. In fact, the trauma of those times helped her sort out what really mattered. With the help of friends and a strong church family, Julia realized that God's desires and expectations for her as a parent were just the same after the divorce as before: her job as a Christian parent was still to raise godly kids. Not only did God want this, she realized, but if she followed biblical principles, she could be confident that He would help it happen. "Regardless of how broken and bruised your family may be," her pastor told her, "the Bible presents absolutely reliable answers that when followed will release God's power to accomplish great things in your family." She's already seeing signs of spiritual growth in both her children.

Julia kept her marriage covenant—an unconditional agreement to be "one flesh till death do us part"—even though her husband didn't. Her friends thought she was crazy, but she's noticed that joy and freedom are the bedrock of her life these days instead of guilt and fear. "God's way works, guys!" she tells her girlfriends, and she holds on to that truth even when discouragement or loneliness crowd in. She's not sure what the future holds, but she says the God of her future has proved Himself trustworthy.

Here's what she wants to see when she looks back on her life: "As for me and my house, we chose to serve the Lord!" She wants her children to remember the effort, purpose, and celebration that went into the making of a Christian family. She wants her kids to remember the sound of her voice praying for them. Despite failures and temporary setbacks, she's resolved to fulfill God's deep desire for her to raise kids who know they're "on mission" for Him in the world.

Marriage, Family, and Chair Two. Ernie is hopeful for his marriage and children. After all, they have everything going for them: solid extended family, a church with a great youth program, financial security. His teenagers seem to spend more time with their non-Christian friends than at home, but their grades are holding up and everybody says they're polite, good kids. Actually, he's pretty sure they're experimenting with drugs and sex, but what can you expect from teens these days? He's hoping they'll stay on track for college educations.

Ernie's marriage seems strong. Not much romance after all these years, to be sure, but not much turmoil either. He and his wife have a good working partnership—kind of a mutual, unspoken contract for success. As long as he keeps the finances in good shape, his wife treats him well. As long as she keeps herself trim, he'll keep his affections at home. To others, they seem the picture of a nice Christian couple.

When others look back on his family, Ernie thinks they'll say, "But as for Ernie and his family, they tried to serve the Lord." He's hoping his kids will remember all the rides to sports practices, and what they learned in camp about their beliefs. He hopes they never noticed how much time he spent down at the station, or that their family's Christianity mostly started when they walked through the church doors and was a little scarce around the house.

Marriage, Family and Chair Three. Kate will get married when she finds a promising candidate and after she's accomplished something to be proud of in her career. She's considering moving in with her current boyfriend to see how things work out. If a relationship isn't positive and convenient, what's the point? she asks. One thing she's sure about: she won't stay in a relationship a minute longer than it's working for her.

She looks forward to having a family and raising children. She already has strong ideas on how to give them every intellectual and social advantage. They're going to be all-around "good kids" and outstanding achievers. But she's already noticed that the parenting advice in most women's magazines tends to change with the times, so she's confused about the details.

Kate wants kids who will remember her as smart, independent, a self-starter, caring, and fun to be around. "Mom knew what she wanted, and that's exactly what she went for!"—that would be a good legacy for any parent.

Now we can round out how life for Julia, Ernie, and Kate looks in the Three Chairs:

HOW THE CHAIRS RELATE TO MARRIAGE AND FAMILY			
	FIRST CHAIR	SECOND CHAIR	THIRD CHAIR
Characteristic	Commitment	Compromise	Conflict
Illustration	Julia	Ernie	Kate
Approach to Marriage:	unconditional covenant	conditional contract	legal convenience
Approach to Parenting:	apply biblical principles; confident	influenced by principles; hopeful	choose own approach; confused
Parenting goal:	raise godly kids	raise good, Christian kids	raise good, successful kids

With careful detail, we have built a portrait of three occupants of the Three Chairs of faith. What I started with was a definition—each Chair stands for a person's spiritual state or level of responsiveness to God. From there we showed how the *consequences* of that spiritual state revealed themselves in the key life relationships—with God, with the world, and within the marriage and family.

By now I hope you see that the distinction between people sitting in each of the Three Chairs is *not* one of degree. For example, Julia isn't a 25 percent better person than Ernie, and so on. What the Chairs show is not shades of value but a fundamental, radical difference. Their lives and choices will never end up at the same place because—in their inner beings—how they see God, value, work, and personal relationships puts them on separate planets!

That means that to get from one Chair to the next requires nothing less than a fundamental, radical spiritual transformation.

Now you can see why Ernie can promise to read his Bible more, or try to persuade his teenagers more, or attend church more—but nothing will change…unless he faces his self-centered, rebellious heart of compromise.

Now you understand why Kate can meditate or help out at the soup kitchen or argue about religion for the rest of her life—but nothing will change…unless a spiritual breakthrough happens at the core of her being.

Now you can see why Julia can expect the curve of her spiritual growth to continue steadily upward toward a deeper, more rewarding relationship with God and a fuller understanding of His wonderful calling on her life.

> *The distinction between people sitting in each of the Three Chairs is not one of degree.*

A STARTLING DISCOVERY

I've saved the most promising and, in some ways, troubling insight about the principle of the Three Chairs for last. In our discussions so far, we've been using the image of the Chairs as seats of commitment to help us understand where our life choices have taken us. Used this way, each Chair works like a snapshot, allowing us to see our spiritual health right now. We're applying the Three Chairs as a *diagnosis*.

But the principle also works as a *dynamic*—that is, it can describe what happens in families over time. It helps us understand how our parents impacted us, and predicts how our Godward commitments (or lack of them) will impact the next generation, and the next.

When we look at where we sit in the Chairs as a generational story, we see the long-term consequences of the diagnosis—and our motivation for spiritual breakthroughs takes on a whole new level of urgency.

The first place in the Bible where I noticed how the Chairs are affected by generations was in the life of Joshua and the two generations which followed him. But here's the startling discovery: I found it again in the stories of Abraham, his son Isaac, and his grandson Jacob. Then I found it expanded in the stories of David, his son Solomon, and his grandson Rehoboam.

As I laid these three different illustrations next to each other, I saw the pattern of the three generations *in every single situation*. Here's how they stack up:

HOW THE GENERATIONS MATCH THE CHAIRS OF FAITH		
FIRST CHAIR	SECOND CHAIR	THIRD CHAIR
commitment	compromise	conflict
Joshua	the elders	the children of the elders
Abraham	son Isaac	grandson Jacob
David	son Solomon	grandson Rehoboam

Perhaps you already noticed this pattern surfacing in our portraits of the Three Chairs. I have to admit, I missed it at first.

What emerges is a pattern of generational slide. That trend from the First Chair to the Second to the Third is inexorably downward and disappointing. The motion seems to push in one direction only—away from First Chair living. If you remember the basics of their Bible stories, you know the outline of these men's lives:

- Joshua, Abraham, and David shared the traits of the First Chair. They know God and have seen His power in their lives. They love and serve Him, and see in their lives the extraordinary blessings that this kind of devotion brings.
- Their children—the elders, Isaac, and Solomon, respectively— present an entirely different set of common traits. They knew what

God had done for their parents and had responded to His truth, but compromise, not commitment, described their spiritual lives. The second generation were all stuck in the Second Chair.

- By the subsequent generation—the third generation described in Judges, Jacob, and Rehoboam—the spiritual index has almost entirely shifted to Third Chair. The details differ, but the overarching theme is one of self-centered decision making and conflict. The legacy they had inherited from their parents was only secondhand news, stripped of all power to pull them toward godliness.

THE TROUBLING PICTURE OF GENERATIONAL SLIDE		
FIRST GENERATION	SECOND GENERATION	THIRD GENERATION
First Chair	Second Chair	Third Chair
knows God	knows of God	knows not God
firsthand faith	secondhand faith	no faith
has "works"	saw the "works"	doesn't believe in "works"
submits to the Bible	respects the Bible	owns a Bible

Taken as a historical pattern, this information is sobering, even hard to believe. The Jews who lived through the conquest of Canaan slipped into Second Chair living? David, the man "after God's own heart," raised a compromiser and backslider in Solomon? Jacob, grandson of the Old Testament's greatest hero of faith, spent most of his life fighting *against* God?

Unfortunately, yes. Good, well-intentioned, God-seeking parents do not automatically succeed in fulfilling God's mandate to raise godly children. I know men and women who sit in the First Chair in their relationship with God whose marriages are anything but First Chair marriages, or whose parenting efforts have resulted in disheartening spiritual outcomes.

After twenty-five years of teaching this material, I've come to some startling conclusions: An overwhelming percentage of children of First Chair parents will come to the point in their lives when they voluntarily choose to trust Christ for their eternal salvation. I'm equally convinced that the vast majority of children of Second and Third Chair people will voluntarily reject the Lord Jesus Christ as their personal savior.

Rather than being intimidated by this evidence, I hope you will be encouraged in your step-by-step progress to claim every arena of your life for God. By now, you realize that which Chair you choose will affect not only your life, but the generations to come.

But friend, even if you're sure by now that you're wedged firmly in Chair Two, it's possible for you to experience the kind of breakthroughs that will get you and keep you seated in the First Chair of faith—and it's possible for your whole family as well. In later chapters we'll talk at length about how to be a First Chair parent and raise godly kids.

Sit in a Chair, Choose a Destiny

How do you feel about the Chair which you are sitting in right now? Do you like it? Are you satisfied with your choice to this point? And, probably most important of all, would you like to spend the rest of your life in that Chair?

The choice for a breakthrough is up to you.

After I preached this message in Houston, a young mother and her fifteen-year-old son stopped me in the parking lot. I noticed she had tears in her eyes, but she wanted to tell me a story. She'd had a difficult life, and spent some of it at a distance from God. But things had turned around.

"Right after the service, I looked over at my son and asked him the tough question, 'Son, which Chair do you think your mother sits in?'" she said. "I could hardly breathe for wondering what he'd say. But I was relieved when he blurted out, 'Mom, you're definitely a First Chair mom! You love God, that's for sure.'" On her face was the smile of a person who hadn't let past failures or old habits become a prison.

When I asked her son where he was sitting, he looked at his mom and thought about it for a minute. "Well, when I was younger, I think I was just sitting on my mother's lap," he said. "But two years ago, I really messed up, big time. Then God really got my attention, and I sold out to Him. So now, I guess I'm just sitting right next to her. We're both sitting right where all the excitement is!"

Friend, dramatic, lasting life change is God's will for your life and for your children's lives. The secret of the Three Chairs is that God is ready with all the spiritual powers of heaven to move you and your family forward to maturity and blessing. Whatever spiritual state you find yourself in right now, nothing less than that is God's will and God's best for you.

If you suspect—or know beyond a doubt—that you're stuck in Chair Two living, you may be feeling doomed to a second-class spiritual life. You may have no idea why you can't experience spiritual breakthroughs. In the next chapter, I want to show you what's keeping some of the nicest, "wisest" people I know from God's amazing destiny for each of us.

Chapter Three

The Pain of the
Man in the Middle

A Closer Look at Chair Two Living

I remember pushing through a crowd at a large Christian conference trying not to lose track of my roommate. I'll call him Bill. Every seminar seemed to have ended at once, and the main lobby was crammed with eager people trying to check out the booths and still get to the next session in time. Suddenly Bill spotted a familiar face across the lobby and he shot ahead, leaving me to follow in his wake.

By the time I caught up with him, Bill and his friend had gotten past the hellos and run smack into an awkward silence. In fact, they just stood there facing each other stiffly, surrounded by a sea of happy noise.

"Bruce, this is Wally," Bill said. "He works in the office next to me back home."

"Wow, that's terrific!" I said and shook Wally's hand. But when I tried to make small talk, it didn't work. The two men seemed to be in shock about something. Maybe back home they didn't get along.

Finally Bill got to the point. "Wally, I didn't expect to see you here." Another awkward pause. "Well, I mean, you're not a Christian, are you?" he asked.

"Yes, I am," said Wally. "But...are you?"

"Sure," said Bill, looking embarrassed. "For thirty years!" Then they both broke out in a big laugh and embraced each other like long lost family members.

On our way to the next session, Bill said something I'll long remember: "I can't believe that. Wally and I have worked next to each other for twenty years, and I never knew he was a Christian until today. I guess we were both undercover." Then he chuckled self-consciously.

That conversation rattled around in my thoughts all day. The more I thought about it, the sadder I became. I kept thinking about the embarrassment of these two Christian men, the awkwardness, the silences. Somewhere in their hearts, too, I was sure, Wally and Bill knew something was terribly wrong with what had just happened.

Take a moment to respond with a yes or no to four questions. I'll call them my "Bill and Wally Quiz":

1. Have you ever heard of an undercover ambassador?
2. Have you ever seen a colorless rainbow?
3. Do you think two brothers who were princes would spend years of their lives together without talking once about their father, the king—the person whose position, wealth, and power explained their own nobility?
4. Is it possible for a person who "has it all" to live as an unhappy beggar in rags?

Okay, how did you do? I'm pretty sure you answered the first three questions with a no. After all, "undercover" and "ambassador," and "colorless" and "rainbow" are oxymorons—words that contradict each other. Impossible. And two brothers in the palace never mentioning Dad, the man on the throne? Not likely.

But what about question four? A rich person in rags? The correct answer there might surprise and sadden you: "Yes. In fact, it happens all the time!"

In this chapter I want to talk more specifically about Christians who live in Chair Two. They're close to my heart, because I used to be one. Chair Two Christians aren't the bad guys. They're not on God's black list. In fact, like Wally and Bill, they fill our Christian conferences with eager faces. They may have gone to church for decades. That sharp dresser who works just down the hall from you might be one.

But the lives of Second Chair Christians, no matter how successful they seem from the outside, are really case studies in loss—colors gone gray and destinies squandered. What you see on the outside might be enviably successful, well-balanced people, but inside they're besieged by doubts and dissatisfactions.

That's why I've titled this chapter about Second Chair Christians, "The Pain of the Man in the Middle." The middle chair is a painful place to call home. Second Chair Christians are neither unrestrained, guilt-hardened pagans nor unfettered, guilt-free Christians. By their own choice, they're caught in a twilight zone. They've traded the joy of following God with a whole heart for the "wisdom" of cutting their own deal—and they've ended up, perhaps without knowing it, as heirs of the king who live like beggars.

The lives of Second Chair Christians, no matter how successful they seem from the outside, are really case studies in loss.

We can safely assume that Wally and Bill weren't First Chair believers. Why? Because if they were, they would have lived every day like believers first, fellow employees second. Their values, convictions, testimony, prayer, passions, and priorities would have leaked out all over their workplace. "Undercover"? Are you kidding! That never works for committed, joyful Christians, even for ones who are as shy as bunnies.

If you're still wondering why I use words like sadness or pain to describe life in the Second Chair, I can tell you that it's because the loss is so great—both to the person and to God's work in our world—and the percentage of those who end up here is so high. By far the highest percentage of today's church-attending Christians are, in my opinion, stuck in Second Chair living.

How could redeemed sons and daughters of God fall so far short of the joy-filled, abundant, overcoming *life* that He promises for those who belong to Him? If you recognize yourself in these descriptions, how could it have happened to you?

Let's take a deeper look at the man or woman in the middle.

A CHEST OF DRAWERS

In the previous chapter we described Ernie, our likable but misguided Second Chair person, with key phrases like:

- saved
- compromised
- motivated by self
- susceptible to guilt
- tends to confuse church activities with vital Christian experience
- marked by inner and outer inconsistencies
- undifferentiated in lifestyle from non-Christians

And now I want to add another identifier:

- compartmentalized

In our culture, we tend to view our lives as a chest of drawers, with a separate drawer for each interest, value, or pastime. One drawer might be for work, another for recreation; one for the "real you" at the gas station, another for the "real you" at a party or a parent-teacher conference. We might have several drawers handy just for church—one for the person we are when we're with the pastor, another for when we're standing in the parking lot after services. For each drawer, we tend to keep handy a separate set of values and a different language.

That's what I mean by "compartmentalized"—the whole is divided into separate, nonoverlapping parts.

When we're living in the Second Chair, we almost always use drawers to keep our life manageable. That should be no surprise. After all, compromise, self-serving, and inconsistency already describe our operating principles. So for every new situation we encounter, we tend to add another drawer to insure complete appropriateness and safety. Rather than having a oneness, an integrity to our character, we play characters.

Of course, to a certain degree, we all show different facets of our personalities, gifts, and interests in different situations. But I'm not talking about facets of the same person, or about the different roles and responsibilities we all must carry as adults. I'm referring to a pervasive lack of consistency or integrity in who the real you is, for better or worse, in every situation.

Compartmentalizing works well if you want to be flexible, uncommitted, maybe even invisible. It's handy if you live in fear, and pure genius if you have lost all hope that there is a genuine, God-created real you anyway.

But if you're trying to reach for all God's best for you, compartmentalizing is a blueprint for a breakdown instead of a breakthrough. How, for example, can you be sure that more than one drawer of your life is really interested in pressing on with God? And what will happen if the you at church makes a decision that the you on the golf course has no intention of honoring?

I have to admit that twenty-first century America seems custom-made for living out of different drawers. Think about it. We hardly know the family next door. We commute to a church miles away, often walking in and out with near anonymity. We work with one crowd and play or pray with another. The opportunities for a little undercover activity are almost limitless. Since no one knows you in any other context, you can reinvent yourself for each one.

And as a society, we've decided that success in one role doesn't have anything to do with what happens in our other roles. Pastors can go through multiple divorces but keep their ministry because they preach well. Politicians can display repugnant personal morals but keep their approval rating because the economy is strong or they vote along party lines.

The most unhappy, frustrated, stressed, and disillusioned people in the world aren't non-Christians as you might expect.

But God has made clear that when He looks at us, He doesn't see rows of compartments or a collection of separate performances. He sees a whole person. Who you are when no one's looking looks just the same to Him as who you are when you are standing in plain view. And God asks for integrity in the lives of His people.

This is why we need to deal with our lives as a whole—and be committed to bringing every arena into the First Chair. For a believer, the convenience of the compartmentalized self is not an option. And anyway, it ultimately fails as a way of life. It's a wisdom built on the sands of hypocrisy. Every Second Chair person discovers soon enough that what started out as a street-smart way to win (even over God's revealed will) ends up as a deep personal loss. Relationships falter under the weight of deceit. Dreams splinter. The spirit withers and eventually admits defeat.

From personal experience I can tell you that the most unhappy, frustrated, stressed, and disillusioned people in the world aren't non-Christians as you might expect, but Second Chair people who know Christ yet who fight Him and His leadership for years and even decades.

Why? Because when compromised believers turn *away* from the Lord and strike a deal with sin, the Holy Spirit convicts and disciplines them so that they'll return. Why wouldn't He? They gave themselves into God's eternal keeping at the moment of salvation. Yet when they try to turn *toward* the Lord to receive His best with only a few parts of their life in agreement (that is, without fully embracing His agenda and His leadership in every "drawer"), they experience only frustration and failure. Of course! God made us with one will, one mind, one heart, one spirit; it is Satan's lie that leaves us fractured and paralyzed.

I believe that what drives a person to a compartmentalized lifestyle more than anything else is this root commitment to using every opportunity and gift God has given you to get the most for yourself. And to get the most return when you're living in between requires that you play a lot of different roles. For Second Chair Christians, this business decision comes into clear focus when we ask ourselves a simple question.

"WHO AND WHAT DO I LOVE?"

To find out if we're caught up in Second Chair living, we should ask ourselves a most telling question: "Who and what do I love most?" By love, I don't mean warm feelings. I mean driving passion, daily motivation, overarching interest, and priority.

Our answer to this seemingly innocent question will divide Christians into two groups who may at first appear alike. For example, both profess to follow and serve the same Lord. Yet the difference between them yawns like the Grand Canyon.

What love really motivates you? Take a look back through your calendar of activities or think back through your week. What were you trying to achieve? What did you dream about? What would your friends say about you? What are you giving your life to achieve? Don't trust your reflex answers or your good intentions—just look at the facts.

Here's how the pattern of the Chairs determines how believers answer the question:

First Chair believers love and are most interested in people. Second Chair believers love and are most interested in something else.

FOR THE LOVE OF PEOPLE

It's true. Whenever First Chair believers are nearby, their love for people is apparent. Whether they are introverts or extroverts, quiet or expressive, humorous or sober, they are always looking for ways to care for the needs of others. They invite people into their homes and get together with them elsewhere. Reaching out is a main theme of their lives.

The early church understood this priority as soon as they took the name of Christ as their identity. When they gathered, Christians shared everything (Acts 2:44–47). If necessary, they sold their possessions to take care of one another. They gave generously to help churches through hard times, unselfishly supporting Paul and other evangelists who took the gospel to an unsaved world. Rather than thinking of their own needs, they thought of other's first—and their own needs were taken care of in the process. The fact that they loved one another so deeply was like a fragrant aroma, drawing others into the family of love (2 Corinthians 2:14–16). Their willingness to humbly serve one another brought them favor with outsiders, who could then be introduced to the God of love.

When you commit to the Lord, you become committed to what He is committed to. That is why First Chair believers love people first.

Did God come to the Garden of Eden to tend His prize-winning grapes or walk in the shade of a landmark elm tree? No, it was to tend His children, Adam and Eve, and to walk and talk in the pleasure of their company.

Did Christ come to rescue business deals, erect public buildings, shore up retirement accounts, write a literary masterpiece, or win a spot on the school board? No, He came to rescue lost people—wonders created in His own image—so that we could have an eternal relationship with Him.

And how much did that commitment mean to him? Most of us have known the truth since childhood:

"God so loved the world that He gave His only begotten Son, that whoever believes in Him should not perish but have everlasting life. For God did not send His Son into the world to condemn the world, but that the world through Him might be saved." (John 3:16–17)

When Jesus spoke of His purpose on earth, He said, "For even the Son of Man did not come to be served, but to serve and to give his life as a ransom for many" (Mark 10:45). Jesus always had time for people, no matter who came to Him. Wherever you turn in the gospels, you cannot escape the fact that the Lord's first love was always for people—people of all races, in all situations, whether powerful or not, acceptable or not, young and beautiful or covered with sores.

We teach our children to sing, "Jesus loves the little children, all the children of the world." Yet some of us have given our children the gold of this insight but kept for ourselves only the rust of doing, achieving, and owning.

Every First Chair Christian has only one choice about who or what matters most: If you embrace the Lord in total commitment, you will embrace his love for others.

FOR THE LOVE OF POSSESSIONS, PLEASURE, POWER, AND PRESTIGE

"Love others most? Sounds fine," says the cautious and perceptive man in the middle. "But as a way of life, I'm not sure. Isn't that what pastors and social workers are for?"

In place of an overriding interest in people goes…something else. After all, all of us pursue what we consciously or subconsciously find significant and appealing. The more appealing something is to us, the more passionate and focused we are about it, and the more we dedicate our thoughts, our time, and our energy to attaining it.

When we're living in the Second Chair, (for obvious reasons) we turn away from God's priorities about loving people. But who can blame us? We've taken our lives back into our own hands and we're trying to succeed, make smart choices, achieve the most with the resources and time we have. What we turn toward, unfailingly, is our own self-interest.

In fact, Second Chair believers have a hard time putting people first in their lives unless they're helping us achieve another priority, like success, pleasure, or status. Reaching out to the needs of people as worthwhile in itself, or simply to honor God's priorities, just doesn't motivate us for long. Soon people are taking a backseat.

"Who or what do you love most?" For the man in the middle, a new set of custom-made set of priorities takes the place of people. His or her driving interests usually fit one of the following categories:

- desire to acquire possessions
- desire for personal pleasure
- desire for power and prestige

But what looks like a winning ticket for the man in the middle turns into ruin. If you don't believe me, just look around you at unhappy Second Chair believers. Just look at one man in the Bible who had everything God above and the earth below could give—and still managed to compromise his life away into destruction and despair.

And, like you and me, he was no dummy. In fact, he was the wisest man who ever lived.

DIARY OF A SECOND CHAIR MAN

His name was Solomon. He grew up as the younger son but favored prince in the sprawling royal family of King David. His mother, Bathsheba, was beautiful, strong, and totally dedicated to steering him safely through the intrigues of court life. His father was already a legend, and looking back, we would quickly pick David as one of the Bible's leading First Chair people.

Crown Prince Solomon—handsome, gifted, wealthy, educated, yet by all early accounts humble and loyal. If you had to pick one person from the Old Testament most likely to succeed in the online, sound bite, big screen world of our times, it would be Solomon. He's the one you'd hire to lead your corporation. To run for public office. To preach. Very likely, to be your personal friend and adviser.

When Solomon became king, the Lord appeared to him in a dream to say, "Ask! What shall I give you?" Solomon's First Chair values are evident in his reply:

> *Can you imagine anyone with a better portfolio for success, both spiritually and materially?*

> Therefore give to Your servant an understanding heart to judge Your people, that I may discern between good and evil. For who is able to judge this great people of Yours?" The speech pleased the Lord, that Solomon had asked this thing. Then God said to him: Because you have asked this thing and have not asked long life for yourself, nor have asked riches for yourself, nor have asked the life of your enemies, but have asked for yourself understanding to discern justice, behold, I have done according to your words…and I have also given you what you have not asked: both riches and honor. (1 Kings 3:9–13)

Can you imagine anyone with a better portfolio for success, both spiritually and materially, than young Solomon? His father's heart for God was legendary. The Lord had gifted him with more wisdom and judgment than any other person in history. And the nation he had inherited was entering its greatest period of peace and prosperity.

What could go wrong?

Something did. And the Bible shows how:

> For it was so, when Solomon was old, that…his heart was not loyal to the LORD his God, as was the heart of his father David. For Solomon went after Ashtoreth the goddess of the Sidonians, and after Milcom the abomination of the Ammonites. Solomon did evil in the sight of the LORD, and did not fully follow the Lord, as did his father David. Then Solomon built a high place for Chemosh the abomination of Moab…and for Molech the abomination of the people of Ammon…so the LORD became angry with Solomon, because his heart had turned from the LORD God Israel. (1 Kings 11:4–9)

What drew Solomon's heart away from all the promise of First Chair living to end his life in the pursuit of pagan gods? I'm convinced that possessions, pleasure, and power came to control his life. He thought he was wise enough to ignore David's final words of advice:

> I go the way of all the earth; be strong, therefore, and prove yourself a man. And keep the charge of the LORD your God; to walk in His ways, to keep His statutes, His commandments, His judgments, and His testimonies, as it is written in the Law of Moses, that you may prosper in all that you do and wherever you turn. (1 Kings 2:2–3)

In an eerie foreshadowing of Solomon's slide, the Law of Moses contained three specific prohibitions for rulers (see Deuteronomy 17:14-20).

- A king should not multiply wealth for himself. (That would be taking advantage of his office for personal gain.)

- A king should not multiply the number of his wives ("lest his heart turn away").
- A king should not multiply horses for himself (lest he become dependent on Egypt, historically the source of fine horses).

But Solomon ignored all three rules.

He Put a Priority on Possessions. Second Chronicles 9:13 records that "the weight of gold that came to Solomon yearly was six hundred and sixty-six talents of gold." That would be almost $4 billion by today's standards.

The problem was that the king acquired wealth for himself. When you desire those things for yourself, you fall into the trap that is woven into the pattern of the Second Chair. Rather than focusing on God, your focus shifts to yourself. Rather than focusing on loving others, your focus shifts to loving yourself. The dangers to your spiritual life are obvious.

He Put a Priority on Personal Pleasure. First Kings reveals that "King Solomon loved many foreign women, as well as the daughter of Pharaoh: women of the Moabites, Ammonites, Edomites, Sidonians, and Hittites—from the nations of whom the Lord had said to the children of Israel, 'You shall not intermarry with them, nor they with you. For surely they will turn away your hearts after their gods.' Solomon clung to these in love." Eventually, he had seven hundred wives and three hundred concubines.

Inexorably, these personal loyalties pulled him into worshiping the gods of his foreign wives and building temples and high places so his wives could worship their idols. By his example, Solomon led the entire nation into idolatry. What started out as a king's right to pursue pleasure turned into active rebellion against God.

He Put a Priority on Power and Prestige. In 1 Kings 4:26, we read, "Solomon had forty thousand stalls of horses for his chariots, and twelve thousand horsemen." In chapter 10 we also read that, "Solomon had horses imported from Egypt…and exported them to all the kings of the Hittites and the kings of Syria." It wasn't that God didn't like horses. He just didn't want the king to put amassing power and status ahead of serving God.

John describes the three main desires of the self that all men and women deal with while on this earth: power, pleasure, and possessions:

> Do not love the world or the things in the world. If anyone loves the world, the love of the Father is not in him. For all that is in the world—the lust of the flesh, the lust of the eyes, the pride of life—is not of the Father but is of the world. (1 John 2:15–16)

In the Garden of Eden, the serpent offered wisdom, tasty food, and a pleasing looking fruit—power, pleasure, and possessions. During the temptation in the wilderness, Satan offered Christ food, wealth, and power—without the cost of obeying God. To that offer, Jesus said no.

To virtually the same one, Solomon, the man in the middle, said yes—too good to pass up.

At that moment, and during countless decisions that followed, Solomon slipped further and further away from Chair One. Why? Because if your answer to "Who and what do you love most?" is anything but loving God and others, you move to Chair Two. Of course, your choice will seem normal, logical, even fool-proof. I'm sure it did to Solomon, too. But each choice will lead to further choices, all going in the wrong direction.

The consequences to Solomon personally and to Israel as a nation were nothing short of disastrous. Solomon ended his life as a practicing pagan. Idol worship became accepted again, even in vogue, in Israel. Solomon's children grew up without any clear sense of their destiny and calling as princes in the historic house of David, the chosen leaders of God's people. The nation groaned under the heavy taxation required to sustain the king's decadent lifestyle. And for all his wisdom, Solomon ended up playing the fool. The king groaned in his old age under the weight of disillusionment and regret...and recorded his misery in the book of Ecclesiastes.

Listen to the pain of the man in the middle:

'Vanity of vanities,' says the Preacher; 'Vanity of vanities, all *is* vanity'.... I, the Preacher, was king over Israel in Jerusalem. And I set my heart to seek and search out by wisdom concerning all that is done under heaven; this grievous task God has given to the sons of man.... I have seen all the works that are done under the sun; and indeed, all *is* vanity and grasping for the wind... (Ecclesiastes 1:2, 12–14)

How Did We Get Here?

If First Chair living is so terrific, and Second Chair living is such a dead end, how does Second Chair living happen, and why is it so common?

I've given this one a lot of thought. If you look at this group carefully, you'll find two kinds of Christians who account for most of the Second Chair crowd.

Casualty #1. The first is the person who started out in the First Chair, then carried on by living mostly on the memory of his conversion (without an ongoing, lively relationship with Christ as Lord), then gradually slid into compromise.

We just witnessed Solomon's slide. We saw the same pattern in the story of the twelve tribes in Judges. They had received victory and the Promised Land. They were ready to finish the conquest within each of their own territories. All that Israel had to do was clean out the pockets of resistance and pagan worship. But as we noted in chapter 2, they failed.

And the story of defeat continues through the tribes of Benjamin, Asher, Naphtali, and Dan all the way to the predictable consequence: "So the children of Israel dwelt among the Canaanites, the Hittites, the

Amorites, the Perizzites, the Hivites and the Jebusites. And they took their daughters to be their wives, and gave their daughters to their sons; and they served their gods" (Judges 3:5–6).

What on earth had happened?

Parental faith must become personal faith for spiritual growth and blessing to be possible.

Rather than committing themselves and completing the task they had been given, the twelve tribes decided to take it easy. They figured they already had most of the land. Understandably, they were tired of fighting. Besides, the people who were living there seemed nice enough. So, perhaps like Wally and Bill in the opening anecdote, the Israelites made a choice: Take the best of both worlds. Straddle the line. Do what seems sensible at the time. Stay undercover if you have to. All of which adds up to a choice to disobey.

Casualty #2. The second way you might find yourself sitting in the Second Chair is that you grew up leaning on the First Chair—and someone moved.

You were raised in a home where you recognized your parents' Christian commitment, and you modeled your life after theirs. But parental faith must become personal faith for spiritual growth and blessing to be possible. When your parents' example strayed off course or you moved out and away from their influence, your own spiritual life lost heat.

Look again at the account of the tribes. What was the difference between Joshua and the elders who outlived him?

- Joshua trusted God (First Chair).
- The elders trusted Joshua, who trusted God (Second Chair).

The elders who outlived Joshua knew the Lord, and they knew of all His great works. Yet by refusing to step across the line of commitment, they were actually rejecting God and His will for them. Instead of driving out the remaining enemies, they made alliances with them. They didn't tear down the altars to false gods, even though they had been told explicitly to do so.

First Chair faith looks at the difficulty of a commitment and calls on the resources of the all-powerful God. Second Chair faith looks at the difficulty and measures what seems practical. Second Chair faith never conquers giants. Second Chair faith never moves mountains.

Eventually, the compromised Christian is leaning so far toward the Third Chair that—as in the case of Wally, Bill, and King Solomon—the outside observer is hard pressed to identify the difference.

Fortunately, this is not the end of the story, especially not your story.

LEAVING THE MIDDLE BEHIND

Perhaps you have recognized yourself in Wally or Bill. Your life suddenly reveals itself as a carefully devised scheme to orchestrate your different interests, desires, and needs (and your faith is just one of these). But now you see the lie of the compartmentalized life. You want to reach for wholeness and integrity and put God first.

Perhaps, like Solomon, you've drifted from a First Chair inheritance into Second Chair ruin for what seemed like the best of reasons: You value your life. You trust your instincts. Most of the time, you try your hardest. But now you have ended up in a spiritual thicket, and the painful consequences of self-centeredness are piling up around you.

My message to you is full of hope. Regardless of what has happened so far in your life, right now you are actually standing on the threshold of breakthroughs you will treasure forever! God will meet you where you are as you come to him in sincerity, honesty, and repentance.

I ask you only these three breakthrough questions:

Do you have the courage to learn and face the truth about God?

Do you have the desire and will to believe the truth?

Are you willing to act on—build the habits and practices of your life upon—what you know and believe?

Then you are ready to leave Chair Two. You are ready for the breakthroughs in the chapters to come.

Remember the opening story of chapter 1? You were squinting into the sun, wondering how you would manage to scale the rock cliff in front of you. The following steps to personal change make up what I call a Breakthrough Toolkit for spiritual climbers. In the breakthrough opportunities ahead, you can use the following guide to help you know where you are and what probably needs to happen next. You may want to bookmark this page so you can return to it easily as you read.

1. Diagnose your situation or problem. To decide if you need a breakthrough in a given area, ask yourself:

- "Is there something I wish were different but I can't seem to change?"
- "Am I stuck in a dry, stagnant place?"
- "Do I repeatedly cave in to a particular sin?"
- "Has God brought a needed change to my attention?"
- "Have other people expressed a wish for me to change?"
- "Do I have a sincere, committed desire to make a change?"

2. Define your breakthrough goal. Be specific. What would a breakthrough in this area look like? How would you think differently? How would you behave or order your life differently? How would you feel differently? How would the new level of living appear to others?

3. Describe the obstacles you face. What stands in your way—a person, obligation, habit, fear, possession, schedule, or attitude? A missing resource? As you name your obstacles, ask God to show which are real and which are not—most obstacles to spiritual breakthroughs are actually based on lies that we take for the truth.

4. Discern the truth. What does the Bible say about this issue? Jesus said that we are set free by truth. No wonder breakthroughs so often come after we have experienced an insight from Scripture, the Holy

Spirit, or a Christian friend. Ask the Lord for wisdom and expect to receive it (James 1:5).

5. Decide to repent and follow through. Most of us struggle to get through to the other side of an unwanted behavior because we're still clinging to something on this side—a pleasurable habit or behavior, a selfish attitude, a wrong desire, a comfortable assumption. Are you willing to let go? Are you willing to be broken? Are you ready to turn away from wrong, make amends, and go in a new direction? If so, you can rest secure knowing that God's love, mercy, and power are now released to bring about the breakthrough you need.

6. Do something to secure your breakthrough. Perhaps the most important step in cementing your breakthrough is to act on it immediately. Peter went out and did the opposite of what he'd done before: Instead of denying Jesus, he proclaimed Him to thousands (see Acts 2). To cement your breakthrough, act on it as soon as you have opportunity. Begin now to implement your breakthrough goals, say no to the lies that have held you captive, say yes to truths that make you free, and move on in your new life in a continual attitude of repentance.

> *Most of us struggle to get through to the other side of an unwanted behavior because we're still clinging to something on this side.*
>
>

MESSAGE TO AN HEIR

How much I wish we could sit together on a park bench on a sunny day and talk. I suppose we'd start by comparing notes on our kids or musing about the weather. We could talk about what you want out of life, what's not coming together for you, and what is. But sooner or later, I'd look you in the eye and deliver my message:

Friend, you are royal. You are favored. You are incredible!

You see, I just imagine if God, your Father, were on that park bench next to you; that's what He'd most like to say. He would see past your struggles, your disappointments, your good intentions, your silly, habitual disasters to the real you—a royal child with a kingdom and a future delivered into your hands.

God never wants you to get so focused on your spiritual problems that you lose sight of the prospects—the unchangeable, God-guaranteed facts about *you*, heir of the king.

You are royal. You are favored. You are incredible!

If you are like so many other struggling Christians I've talked to at moments like this, you may be a wounded prince or princess who is carrying a proof around in your heart or memory every day that God is not reliable. That He's not loving or strong. That proof is an unresolved hurt or disappointment, a perceived failure, or very real grief that keeps your heart and will locked up.

Your heavenly Father, the king, has brought you to this page, my friend, to this earnest exchange on a park bench. Only Satan wants you to believe that your Father is not utterly and eternally trustworthy to be Lord of your life. Only Satan wants you to believe the lie that spiritual maturity is some vast or mysterious thing only possible for certain Christians with special spiritual aptitude.

As you follow Him, God will lead you toward wholeness and love. His Spirit will gently, firmly guide you into opportunities to choose to put Him first. These are moments of destiny, because each choice will move you forward into Chair One—or leave you stuck in the middle.

I can tell you from personal experience that letting go of your personal agenda is perhaps the hardest thing you will ever do. But by your will and effort, and carried forward by God's tremendous power at work in you, your grip on the old, compromised way of life will lessen. One finger at a time you will let go to God....

And begin to receive the amazing kingdom life you were created for in the first place.

Experiencing Breakthroughs with God

Chapter Four

Deep~Sea Decisions

BREAKING THROUGH TO SERVING GOD

The adventure started with a sleek private jet waiting on the runway for me and my son. Johnny, a wealthy friend, had a plan for the next two days, and when Johnny gets a plan in his head, nothing stops him. That explained why his pilot was there in Atlanta escorting us on to Johnny's corporate jet.

We were going deep-sea fishing.

Johnny makes things happen like that. He stands tall, dresses like a million bucks, and never has to leave home without a tan. What a life! With just a phone call, managers jump. Money flows. Deals fizzle or fly. To me, it always looked like Johnny had the world at his fingertips.

With less effort than it takes me to get my lawn mower started—or so it seemed—we were ushered smoothly from jet to luxury sedan to motor yacht. Early the next morning, Johnny was navigating his twin-engine vessel past the buoys in the direction of his favorite offshore fishing spot.

"You're going to catch fish 'til you drop!" he promised, keeping one eye glued on his state-of-the-art navigational computers.

He was right. Hours later, my son and I could hardly lift a can of soda. We'd spent every ounce of strength pulling in trophy-sized fighting fish. It had been a day of watching tuna and amberjacks send the line screaming from our reels and leave us panting for breath before they finally lay there, flapping heavily on deck.

During the long ride back in the setting sun, Johnny and I stood at the stern talking. He's a good friend, but I'd known for some time that his Christian commitments were compromised and that he most likely sat in the Second Chair. Our conversation turned to spiritual things.

"Johnny," I began, "do you think you have enough money?" He didn't take offense at the question, but he was still surprised.

"Well, I suppose so," he said. "I've never thought about it. I mean, how would you ever know if you had enough money?"

I listened for a moment to the mighty engines thrumming under my feet. Then I ventured a reply. "Well, could you live at your current lifestyle with the money or investments you have for the rest of your life—without working another day?"

It was obvious he'd never thought about this question. After a few moments, he said, "Well, now that you put it that way, the answer is yes. I have enough money right now."

Sensing the Lord's prompting, I looked my friend squarely in the eyes and asked, "Well, if that's true, why don't you draw a line in your bank account and from now on give every single dollar more that you earn to the Lord's work?"

Johnny looked like he'd taken a hard punch to the jaw. He staggered back, leaning against the rail. He stroked his brow. "But, Bruce, if I gave it all away," he finally sputtered, "what would I have to live for?"

There it was. The truth, laid out on his deck like a prize fish. The man who had seemed to have everything at his command was actually caught himself in the grip of another master.

As the sunset colors glowed and we powered toward home, the conversation took Johnny deeper. For the first time in his life, he finally faced the Joshua Challenge: "Choose for yourself whom you will serve."

Up to now, Johnny admitted, he'd chosen to serve money and the pursuit of money. His god demanded his time, his energies, his sweat, his thoughts—and no matter how successful he became, no matter how much he *seemed* the master of his circumstances, his god never had enough. Consequently, no room remained for him to experience a deeper, more significant relationship with the Lord.

Years have passed, and this is what I remember about that deep-sea excursion: the sound of big, slippery fish hitting the deck, the ache in my arms, and a trophy man who stood beside me in the sunset and chose another master.

These days, you'd never recognize Johnny. He's still a whiz at business, but what comes first for him is serving the Lord. If you were to ask Johnny which master brings the most meaning, satisfaction, sense of significance, joy, and blessing, he wouldn't hesitate. He'd smile, ask you to sit down, and unreel his favorite fishing story.

The one where the Lord of life reached down and caught his heart.

WHOM DO YOU SERVE?

That day Johnny experienced a breakthrough about serving that was so fundamental it immediately transferred him from Second Chair faith into First Chair faith. In our quest for spiritual breakthroughs, we too will have to face the question of who's in charge in our life and whom and what we really serve.

Facing this question, which is at the heart of the Joshua Challenge, is never easy. Some of us keep running up on the rocks over this issue for years, if not our entire lifetimes.

In fact, this chapter might make some of you feel like someone just threw a punch to your jaw. Until now, you thought your

In our quest for spiritual breakthroughs, we too will have to face the question of who's in charge in our life and whom and what we really serve.

Christian walk was about how God could help you get what you want—how your life could be better, safer, happier than the pagan's next door. Suddenly you realize that you're probably still floundering on the rocks of who is master of your life.

The bottom line in any committed relationship with God is this: *Who will be master, and who will be servant?* Or put it this way: *Will I allow God to be God in my life?*

This truth about serving God is difficult to market on infomercials, let me tell you. It doesn't have much entertainment value or glitter appeal. And face it, our call to complete surrender in God's service has zero in common with our right to pursue the American Dream.

But spiritual breakthroughs with God start here—for you and me, just like they did for Johnny.

Remember the story of Peter? As a struggling disciple who was trying to have it both ways, Peter failed miserably. (That's the problem with Chair Two, by the way: neither your faith nor your personal life really works. One will always compromise and hinder the other.) He called Jesus "Master," but the master he served was his own impulses.

But Peter didn't stay in the Second Chair. By the end of his life, he was proclaiming not just that Jesus was the Messiah, but that *Jesus is Lord!"*

All through the letters of the apostles you'll find the proof that each man had faced the Joshua Challenge—and knelt before Christ. Time and again, these former Second Chair believers, now respected leaders of a movement that was shaking the known world, chose one key word for their job titles:

"Paul, a *servant* of Christ…" (Romans 1:1).

"James, a *servant* of God and of the Lord Jesus Christ…" (James 1:1).

"Simon Peter, a *servant* and an apostle of Jesus Christ…" (2 Peter 1:1).

You see, once we settle the question of who will be master, we have absolute clarity on how we must approach and relate to God. As servant. That means that when we come to the Lord seeking breakthroughs, we won't get anywhere if we're trying to retain a position of power or trying to maneuver and bargain for what we want.

For each of us, the question of lordship will be like the Great Wall of China across the path of our spiritual growth until the question is faced and resolved as God requires. We may experience different break-throughs—in our prayers, in serving others, in knowledge. But the over-riding breakthrough that gets us from Chair Two to Chair One hinges on our decision to serve Him.

As you would expect, serving the Lord involves more than external actions. It also involves our internal attitudes—having a heart and mind that are set on pleasing Him.

Fortunately for us as God's children, Jesus told us in one memorable sentence what it means to treat Him as Lord and pursue His agenda alone. This breakthrough sentence shimmers just under the surface of one of Jesus' sermons like a diamond in the water, like a gleaming trophy fish.

The Secret under the Surface

Well, I haven't told you Johnny's secret for catching the really big fish. As in every other area of his life, Johnny set out to win. When it came to sport fishing off the Florida coast, he and his friends had "cracked the code." While we sped out to the fishing grounds that morning, he told me all about it.

They had picked a promising shoal offshore and over time turned it into something of a junkyard. That's right. Each trip out, they'd hoist aboard chunks of wrecked cars, old appliances, any kind of industrial structure. Then, using satellite-guided navigation gear, they'd return to the same coordinates and drop their cargo overboard. In time they had created their own reef—a perfect home for a rich variety of sea creatures and the big sport fish that preyed on them.

And it worked. Johnny didn't have to wander blindly around the ocean hoping fish would find his boat. He went straight to the designated trophy spot where he knew he'd find what he was seeking.

Friend, let me take you to my favor trophy spot for growing Christians—Matthew 6:33. So many seekers (spiritual fisherman) wander through Bible waters pointing to a good principle here, a strong character value there. Somehow they expect to be transformed. But they never find the secret of serving God—and the spiritual breakthrough that it promises. It lies there just under the surface for every seeking heart. Jesus says: "But seek first the kingdom of God and His righteousness, and all these things shall be added to you."

Let me break down the verse word by word and phrase by phrase so we can examine it more carefully for clues to serving God.

The word "seek" defines my starting point. "Seek" is an action verb; it's something you do. The word means to "go in search for; to try to discover; to try to acquire or gain." When Johnny goes out deep-sea fishing, he's clearly looking for something—all his focus is on seeking a big fish, and he knows where to look. In the same way, we seek God where He can be found—in the Bible, in the words of others, in prayer. In fact, He promises us that if we will seek Him, we will find Him.

The word "first" defines the priority that I must give to this action. Something that is first in priority has the highest rank and the supreme position. When we prioritize, we purposely give preferential treatment to what matters most. When our priorities get out of whack, we end up serving something or someone other than God, and we slide into Second Chair living.

"His kingdom" defines for me what I am to seek or to achieve. And there's not much wiggle room here. Think of the kingdom as the King's agenda.

Have you ever worked on a group project that seemed to keep getting off track? The problem can often be traced back to a person or people who insist that they have the group's goals in mind, but whose actions and emphasis make it clear that they're actually pursuing their own, private agenda.

When a person seeks "His kingdom," he invests his life to further what the *Lord* wants accomplished on this earth.

You can't miss the two most important objectives that Jesus puts on the agenda for His kingdom (see especially Matthew 28:19–20):

1. To evangelize everyone in the world with the wonderful gospel of Jesus Christ, so that they will believe on Him and receive salvation.

2. To disciple all believers in the world to obey all that the Bible teaches so that we are all conformed fully into the image of Jesus Christ.

Serving God finds its purpose for others when we bring them truths of the kingdom.

"His righteousness" defines the kind of person I am to become. His righteousness is my second priority. While seeking His kingdom emphasizes His rule, His righteousness emphasizes His character. The first is what I seek to achieve for the Lord; the second is what I seek to become in the Lord. Jesus isn't talking here about the blameless righteousness that covers me as my salvation gift, but of the Christlikeness which grows in the life of the believer who strives for maturity and holiness.

In fact, Jesus devotes the majority of His Sermon on the Mount to outlining point by point these specific acts of righteousness—prayer, fasting, giving, and so on. When we actively seek to expand His life in ours, His character gradually becomes ours.

Now we have a working description of what it means to "serve the Lord": We are seeking and practicing His agenda uppermost, striving all the while to become more like Him.

Sounds simple. So why do so many of us flounder?

I've thought a lot about why so few Christians stay at the foot of the cross, choosing to serve God and his kingdom first and only. I've turned my own life inside out and upside down to find answers. If Jesus was so clear about what it meant to serve him, why do so many of us still fall away, unable to make that leap to abandoned faith?

If Jesus was so clear about what it meant to serve him, why do so many of us still fall away, unable to make that leap?

My conclusion is that we are done in by delusions.

KINGDOM DELUSIONS

Jesus first made his stirring announcements of the kingdom of God to wild acclaim, excited crowds, and disciples by the score. Remember? All those dusty, disease-ridden, heartsore Jews were sure they'd found the answer at last. Yes, this Jesus would restore the kingdom and the power to Israel—and kick out the Roman oppressors.

And then came the official opposition.

And then came troublesome teachings from the Messiah himself—lines like, "If anyone desires to come after Me, let him deny himself, and take up his cross daily..." (Luke 9:23).

And then came arrest, a sham trial, and finally a humiliating crucifixion.

When the time of death arrived, the curious crowds had already drifted home. Above the victim's bloody head, a public notice fluttered in the wind: "This is Jesus, King of the Jews."

What had happened to the kingdom of God? Apparently, it was gone. Probably it was only a delusion....

Can't you imagine yourself, a spiritual pilgrim, looking up into the kind, broken face of that dying man and asking the same question? And then turning away? I can. I think I could have walked away that day determined never to get fooled again.

I believe thousands of Christians have done exactly that. How painful and potentially offensive it is for me to say this! Like those simple seekers two millennia ago, the majority of us follow Christ happily as long as the promise and the rewards *we* have in mind hold out.

We cling to our own kingdom delusions. They have nothing to do with the reality of Christ's kingdom and everything to do with what we're looking for, and how we go about finding it.

Here's how it happens:

1. We're Fooled by the Clock

If I met you in heaven one hundred years from today, I know what you'd be doing. Here's the preview:

> And there shall be no more curse, but the throne of God and of the Lamb shall be in it, and *His servants shall serve Him*. They shall see His face, and His name shall be on their foreheads…and they shall reign forever and ever. (Revelation 22:3–5)

The clock fools us completely when we lose sight of eternity.

> After these things I looked, and behold, a great multitude which no one could number, of all nations, tribes, peoples, and tongues, standing before the throne and before the Lamb, clothed with white robes, with palm branches in their hands, and crying out with a loud voice, saying, "Salvation belongs to our God who sits on the throne, and to the Lamb!".… *They are before the throne of God, and serve Him day and night in His temple*. And He who sits on the throne will dwell among them. (Revelation 7:9–10, 15)

I love those verses! They tell me that our eternal future will be an outpouring of ecstatic joy in love, praise, and service of our King. Amazingly enough, in the new life, "serving" God and "reigning" with Him will be impossible to tell apart. And He who sits on the throne will dwell among us!

You see, the clock fools us completely when we lose sight of eternity—and remember we were created as eternal beings. We discard our identity. We forget God's timeline. All we see is now, all we hear is *tick, tick, tick,* and Jesus' kingdom seems like an illusion.

But it's real. A billion years more real than that clock.

2. What We Worship Isn't God At All

When we go back to Joshua 24, we see Joshua naming the number one obstacle to serving God: idolatry.

He says, "Put away the foreign gods which are among you" (v. 23).

No matter where I travel around the world, I see how idolatry keeps people out of the First Chair. It may be the love of money or the love of things which drive a person away from God. For others, it might be a relationship that's become a god they can't give up. Or perhaps they worship power, and so they work one hundred hours a week.

How do you know when you are serving an idol? Ask "What and whom do I spend my time, money, and talents on?" Is it the clock, your checkbook, your kids? Is it your boss?

The breakthrough that must occur in the heart of a man and the heart of a woman usually doesn't occur until their idol has been toppled—and they begin to truly worship the King.

3. We Miss God's Good Intentions

The third delusion centers upon the fact that we are afraid that we will lose our lives if we serve God. We think that all joy and happiness will soon disappear if we turn our lives over to His rule. We are sure that the moment we really say to the Lord, "I'll do anything You want; I'll go anywhere You say," He will immediately hand us a ticket to a slow boat to the most remote location in the world, where we will fade away into complete oblivion.

At the root of this delusion is the lie that the Lord doesn't value our lives and that once we "give Him full control," He will treat us with such disdain and carelessness that we'll wander forever in the wilderness of futility.

On the other hand, we reason, if we can only remain in control and determine our own destiny—which obviously require our keeping His hands off our lives (except maybe on Sunday morning)—then we'll surely know how to make our lives turn out and have the most meaning and purpose.

But consider Jesus' words: "For whoever desires to save his life will lose it, but whoever loses his life for My sake and the gospel's will save it"; and, "For what will it profit a man if he gains the whole world and loses his own soul?" Mark 8:35–36

Christ goes right for the jugular when He says that anyone who desires to save his life is ultimately going to lose it. In fact, Jesus teaches that they will be the very ones who will have wasted their lives!

Now comes the challenging part and the miraculous answer that Christ revealed in His Sermon on the Mount. If a person were to devote more and more of his time and effort into serving Christ's kingdom, who would take care of everything else? Jesus anticipated that very issue in the lives of those who seek first His kingdom and righteousness:

> "Therefore do not worry, saying, 'What shall we eat?' or 'What shall we drink?' or 'What shall we wear?' For after all these things the Gentiles seek. For your heavenly Father knows that you need all these things. But seek first the kingdom of God and His righteousness, and all these things shall be added to you." (Matthew 6:31–33)

Jesus makes the contrast unmistakable, doesn't He? If you seek first His kingdom, then His Father will add every single one of those things to you. The Father knows everything you need, and the Father will give it to you. When you change agendas, you also change bosses, from you to Him. He assumes the full responsibility to take care of all of your needs "according to His riches in glory."

In other words, change bosses and the benefit package of the new management will include everything you could possibly need.

SPRINGBOARDS TO KINGDOM SERVICE

Do you want a practical place to start? After all, one of the most important parts of the breakthrough process is taking action. Serving God in your head is a good intention not a life change. Serving God is about doing—doing with every fiber of your passion and commitment.

Here are a few springboards you can use at any time to take another step closer to total commitment to Christ and His kingdom.

1. Devote More of Your Time to the Kingdom

Financial consultant Ron Blue often says that you can tell a person's values by just glancing at two little books: his checkbook and his appointment book. He's right. The starting place of "seeking first" is always your time—even your earning power begins here.

> *The starting place of "seeking first" is always your time.*

The most common mistake for people trying to make a change in time priorities is to jam something else to do into an already overbooked life. But that approach will only set you up for failure. Instead, take about an hour and track through how you spent your time during the past week. Look at blocks of one hour. Something has to get the ax, because to put something more important in, something less important has come out. So, pick up the handle and take a calculated swing.

One of our friends decided to take on the responsibility of teaching a Sunday school class. The only time he had to prepare is from 5:00 to 8:30 each Sunday morning. Something important—sleep—went out the window to make room for something better. (He says he now rigidly guards his Sunday afternoon naps!)

Are you ready to invest an hour a week directly into the kingdom? Then identify what can go and make the change. My guess is that soon you'll find your heart pulling you more and more into kingdom activities. Here are a few new time commitments friends have made with great success:

- negotiated a four-day/ten-hour work week so he can devote Fridays to ministry;
- downsized their lifestyle by selling their large home and moving into a smaller one, so he can work 20 percent less each week;
- used their summer vacation for a missions trip;
- took in an unwed mother who had no place to stay.

If you're motivated, the Lord will help you find the time to fulfill His command. In fact, watch out for miracles.

2. Donate More of Your Treasure to the Kingdom

Jesus taught that your heart and your treasure can always be found in the same spot (Matthew 6:21). The practical application is obvious: If you want your heart to move deeper into the kingdom living, then purposefully invest your treasures there and your newly moved treasures will draw you right to them! But there's an additional principle at work: Your heart moves toward your treasure to the same degree you had to sacrifice to put it there. If your donation didn't really cost you much then not much of your heart is going to follow it.

Sometimes our greatest treasures are worth the smallest amounts of money. Here are some favorite treasure stories on my list:

- a woman gave another her most prized oil painting;
- a family gave their second car to a needy working mom;
- a man gave away all of his clothes except what he wore on his back;
- a couple gave their entire retirement account;
- a teenager gave her Christmas money;
- an executive gave his prized fountain pen to an unemployed and discouraged friend.

And the list goes on: stuffed animals, furniture, frequent fliers' mileage points, a trip to the beach won in a contest, wedding jewelry, a kidney for a dying sister. I wish you could know seven "bald" men I met—they shaved off all their hair in support of a dying friend who had lost his hair to cancer.

Can you see how kingdom living is full of surprises and marked by joy? This kind of service to God makes us rich.

And remember Jesus teaching that a secret of giving isn't merely the *amount* but the *degree* of our sacrifice. You don't have to have millions like Johnny to become a huge giver. When the poor widow put the smallest coin possible in the temple offering, Jesus told startled onlookers that she had given more than anyone else that day—because she had given all that she had.

3. Donate More of Your Talent to the Kingdom

Every Sunday, extremely gifted and competent women, men, and youth walk into churches across this world and mysteriously slide into the Passive Zone. During the week at work, they apply all of their effort, skills, and creativity for a paycheck. But once they're inside church, they suddenly turn inept. "But I'm not very good at anything," they'll mumble. Or, "I'd rather just watch." Or, "I tithe, so I don't really need to get involved, do I?"

The more we're committed to seeking the growth and health of the kingdom of God, the more we will want to apply everything that we are and can do to Christ's work. It's simply good stewardship.

Take a moment for some introspection. What would the people who know you the best say you are best at doing?

1. My greatest strength/skill is _____.
2. My second best strength/skill is _____.
3. My third best strength/skill is _____.

Now take this personal exam just one step further: What percentage of each of these strengths/skills are you currently using to further the kingdom of God? I don't mean the percentage of your time, but how much of the real you in talents, passions, and training are you dedicating to the kingdom? Write down your estimate.

If you're open, the Holy Spirit will start to bring some new, meaningful opportunities to mind.

4. Develop Your Skills through Training for the Kingdom

Besides sleeping and working, we spend more time in our life training than anything else. Just consider the years you have spent in school and professional training programs. Skills-training helps us get maximum results for what we want to achieve. At Walk Thru the Bible, we have trained over 100,000 teachers and pastors to communicate more effectively. Every year, we sponsor an intense in-house training, The Institute for Excellence, to further each team member's skills.

Why do smart organizations invest so much in training? Because the organization benefits many times over in increased productivity, better quality, and a happier work force. The same principles should be applied in our spiritual lives. The Bible teaches that God wants all of us to produce good works and much fruit for Him in our lifetimes.

Think of the training opportunities that would help you serve God more effectively and with greater fulfillment: Christian books, seminars, audiotapes, videos or DVDs, evening school at a nearby seminary or Bible college, and the many emerging Internet resources.

Resolve to stay a lifelong learner and keep at it until He calls you home. Set realistic but challenging goals, and write down how you will accomplish them before December 31.

5. Dream More of Your Special Task in the Kingdom

Many of us languish in apathy and disinterest about serving the Lord because we're not driven by a compelling awareness of the Lord's purpose for us. People I've met who serve God with the most zest and confidence do so because they have a clear sense of destiny in their lives. I'm not talking about some kind of dreamy conviction that dropped into their lap during one prayer time or a walk in the woods. Rather, they're absolutely certain that what they are doing with their lives is eternally important and significant.

People I've met who serve God with the most zest and confidence do so because they have a clear sense of destiny in their lives.

That certainty brings focus and meaning. It helps them determine what's irrelevant, unproductive, and off target for them. Like Paul, they sense they live inside God's grip—and they're holding on, too.

Paul described his personal certainty as "laid hold of" by God. He lived in God's grip—and he, too, was holding on with all his might. This awareness that God was up to something important, personal, and unique in his life was a key ingredient in Paul's incredible, lifelong energy in Christ's service. Here's how he described it: "Not that I have already attained, or am already perfected; but I press on, that I may lay hold of that for which Christ Jesus has also laid hold of me" (Philippians 3:12).

Do you see the power in those words? "I press on to grasp and own for myself that life for which Jesus has grasped and owned me!" God lays hold of you—you lay hold of God. It's the dynamo of personal destiny spinning inside every sold-out servant of God.

Friend, it's true—the Lord has laid hold of you just as He laid hold of Paul. Keep this dream alive in your heart. Ask God to help you see your task, know it, and seize it more every day. And as you keep bringing your priorities and activities in line with your special task in Christ's kingdom, your service for him will explode with vitality, fulfillment, and results.

FISHING FOR THE PRIZE

Has the master/servant question kept you in Chair Two? I hope this chapter has brought some clarity and conviction into your spirit. I pray with all kindness that you have arrived at a breaking point—that you have knelt or want to kneel before your great and loving Master.

This is the spiritual breakthrough where you lose your life—in order to save it.

There's no other way.

And there's no other way with such reward, either. Paul called it the "prize of the call." Your fisherman friend, Peter, described it as the "inexpressible and glorious joy" he found in serving God (read 1 Peter 1:1–9 for details).

Realize that you may flounder for a while in the transition process. That's okay. Up to now in your life, if you've served your agenda first, then you've built a whole way of life around it. As your old priorities die before the Lord and His agenda, you may go through a period when your life may not seem as exciting or meaningful as before—tempting you to return to your old ways.

Don't misinterpret that experience! It's only withdrawal pains from the drug of self-seeking. Ask the Holy Spirit to carry you through this intermediary, desert period until you touch the Promised Land on the other side. Refocus your eyes on the Lord, who stands right before you at all times, ever-beckoning you to further steps and stages of faithfulness.

Your perseverance in seeking God is precious to Him—please remember that. Even your recurring struggles, flailing, arguing, and doubts. Because God is at work in you, my friend. His heart is always *for* you, and His loving and very specific purposes for you have been set from eternity past. That's why serving God with all your heart, with all your time, and with all your gifts is a breakthrough that will give you what you've been looking for:

Your destiny.

I think I can see it rising through blue water. It's huge, I'm telling you! It's pulling hard on the end of your line. Your arms are aching. Your back is burning. But don't let go. Johnny's yelling encouragement. Peter's laughing, shouting, "Hang on!"

There it is, breaking the surface. The trophy of a lifetime, and it's all yours.

Chapter Five

The Monster in the Garage

BREAKING THROUGH TO A CLEAN HEART

A few weekends ago, it finally got to me. It had gotten to my wife long before that, and even the dog had started growling at the sight.

My very own garage monster.

For me the awakening happened the day I drove up to the house, opened the garage door, and realized that I might just have to leave the car in the driveway. Permanently.

Looming before me was a threatening pile of boxes; half-empty paint cans; dusty bicycles with flat tires; full recycling bins; unglued, unbolted, and unfinished repair projects; the trunk of Christmas decorations still waiting to get into the attic; a drifting or two of leaves from last fall; and one lime green water pistol. Rumor had it that two neighborhood children had vanished in its catacombs without a trace. Mice had moved in.

And now the car would have to move out.

That embarrassing possibility turned out to be the final push I needed. I took a big breath and went to work cleaning, sorting, storing, and throwing away. You know, once I settled in to taking care of the junk in there, the garage started looking better in no time.

Sound familiar? Why in the world do we let junk pile up like that? Maybe it all seems indispensable at the time. Or maybe we're just too lazy or hurried to dispose of things properly. Soon we have a monster on our hands and we've run out of wiggle room.

Sin in our lives is like that. Little and big, sins add up one selfish decision at a time; one misplaced priority at a time; one rebellion at a time. Soon we have a scary stockpile of sins that threatens to do us in. And in the process, we've gotten off track with God, and His voice has become increasingly distant and unfamiliar.

Accumulated and unaddressed sin is the primary force that pulls us out of the First Chair and chains us firmly in the Second Chair.

You—a responsible, caring, seeking Christian—with a sin problem? Yes.

Me—a seminary-educated Bible teacher and Atlanta Braves fan—a sinner? Certainly.

If you're like most Christians, at this very moment, you have sins in your life from the past that are spoiling your Christian experience. Or you have present sins you commit either regularly or sporadically that you've given up on trying to deal with. Perhaps reluctantly, you've allowed them to become part of the interior picture of your life, like furniture or wallpaper.

In the last chapter, we discussed what it meant to serve the Lord. I hope you experienced breakthroughs in your commitment to put Him and His kingdom first. But if you couldn't seem to take that leap, if something still holds you back, my guess is that sin is involved. In fact, if you asked me how often a stockpile of sin is the reason Christians can't break through to serving God or connecting meaningfully with Him, my answer would be "nearly 100 percent of the time."

Even if you *are* serving God and sitting in the First Chair of faith, you still need this chapter. Accumulated and unaddressed sin is the primary force that pulls us out of the First Chair and chains us firmly in the Second Chair. After Joshua challenged the Israelites to choose to serve the

Lord, he told them to "put away the foreign gods which are among you." He was asking them to take another look at anything in their lives they worshiped or served apart from God. Anything that was contrary to His will and His ways. In other words, anything that was sin.

God was saying, "You can't serve me without putting away that which comes between us." The only way for any of us to remain in the Chair of commitment is to pursue holiness with the Lord and learn how to see, face down, and clean up the sins in the farthest corners of our heart.

THE MAKING OF A STOCKPILE

We usually think of a stockpile positively: a pantry is a stockpile of food; a silo is a stockpile of grain. But in the Christian life, the biggest and most common stockpile is one of sin. Not one kind of sin but many; not just recent sins but those committed over years and even decades; not merely little no-nos but ruinous and far-reaching disasters; not only private disobediences, but public failures.

Please understand I'm not talking to you about sin that would *eternally* separate you from God. If you're a Christian, you've placed your whole trust in God for His forgiveness and His promise of eternal life. No sin can separate you from your salvation because Jesus died for every single one of those sins—past, present, and future.

To prevent confusion, we need two terms for two kinds of forgiveness:

1. *Salvation forgiveness* occurs only once, at the time of conversion when the Lord forgives the person's sins; gives him eternal life; transforms him from being an enemy of God to a child of God; sends the Holy Spirit into his life as a seal until the day of redemption; and brings about many other one-time changes as recorded in the New Testament.

2. *Fellowship forgiveness* should occur repeatedly throughout the life of every believer. Why? Every time born-again believers sin (and all of us sin before and after salvation), we're instructed in the Bible to confess our sins. Our ongoing, wayward behaviors don't threaten our eternal future

with God, but they do pollute and weaken our ability to fully serve, respond to, and enjoy Him in the present.

You see, every sin grieves the Lord and to some degree affects our relationship with Him. It is for that very reason that He instructs us to confess our sins to Him—so that our relationship can remain in harmony; so that His fatherly discipline of us can end; so that our life can return to holiness in all of its parts; and so that the enemy will no longer have opportunity to afflict us and thwart God's plan.

Perhaps that's why the apostle Paul offers this warning to all believers:

Likewise you also, reckon yourselves to be dead indeed to sin, but alive to God in Christ Jesus our Lord. Therefore do not let sin reign in your mortal body, that you should obey it in its lusts.… Do not you know that to whom you present yourselves slaves to obey, you are that one's slaves whom you obey, whether of sin to death, or of obedience to righteousness. (Romans 6:11–12, 16)

Many Christians these days have reacted against the piety and religious rigidity of earlier times. Even the word *sin* has fallen out of favor. Christians seem to see themselves as floating along safely in a sea of grace. As long as they're doing their best, God's mercy will take care of the rest.

Yet this is a limited—and very convenient—view of what the Christian walk is meant to be. God never winks at sin. And apart from God's intervention, we never escape its consequences. Maybe that's why the Bible clearly states that we have a continuing role and responsibility to deal with sin and to "cleanse ourselves."

Consider these words of advice from Paul:

Nevertheless the solid foundation of God stands, having this seal: …"The Lord knows those who are His…and,…Let everyone who names the name of Christ depart from iniquity.…

Therefore if anyone cleanses himself…he will be a vessel for honor, sanctified and useful for the Master, prepared for every good work. (2 Timothy 2:19, 21)

There's no confusion in these two verses regarding who is supposed to do the action of "cleansing"—it is every person "who names the name of Christ."

This cleansing—or need for fellowship forgiveness, as we've called it—is not a once-for-all act, but an ongoing process leading to more and more holiness of life, which the Bible describes as "perfecting holiness." As 2 Corinthians 7:1 says, "Beloved, let us cleanse ourselves from all filthiness of the flesh and spirit, perfecting holiness in the fear of God."

Confession and cleansing are among the most difficult disciplines to practice.

Over the years, I have struggled to understand and then apply this concept of taking responsibility for cleansing myself of known sin. Although it may look simple, it isn't easy. In fact, I have found that confession and cleansing are among the most difficult disciplines to practice. For most us, even the idea of dealing with our sin is about as appealing as having a tooth drilled—or cleaning out a garage.

In both cases, the longer we wait to deal with it, the more cost and discomfort we're likely to face. With this in mind, it's time to stop staring in dismay at that stockpile and take action.

TAKING ON THE STOCKPILE

Imagine you're standing in the middle of the garage. You have a plan. The Dumpster is ready. Now I'm going to provide you with a powerful tool that you can use to clean out your stockpile anytime you need to. I have taught thousands these steps toward cleansing from sin, and I can promise you two things: 1) First, they work, and they will work for you—

every time, without exception; 2) Second, the process is not easy, but the results are overwhelmingly wonderful.

Step 1: Admit You Have a Stockpile of Sin

The first step toward godly change is always the same—face the truth and diagnose the situation. Practically, this means you no longer:

1) avoid the truth;
2) rationalize away what you know is a problem;
3) remain defensive about why you shouldn't do what you know is right.

In my experience, the condition of our own stockpile of sin is already known to us. Why? Because God is always in communion with us, His children. It is we who, like stubborn preschoolers, cover our ears to what we don't want to hear. But from the moment we first stray, the Holy Spirit is always present, whispering, patiently urging, naming the problem, turning on the light of truth, and convicting us to make a change.

This part is all bad news, and it hurts to admit how expert we have become at denial. To break out of this rut, we must be completely honest and admit that we indeed have a significant problem of sin that we've stuffed just under our consciousness, but that now we're determined, by the Lord's mercy and grace, to deal with it.

Step 2: Believe That You Can Enjoy a Completely Clean Heart

Don't forget the good news. In fact, we can get stuck before we even get started and lose all measure of motivation if all we see is our need. That's why John reminded believers to embrace both sides of the truth about cleansing:

Side one: "If we confess our sins..."

Side two: "He is faithful and just to forgive us our sins and to cleanse us from all unrighteousness" (1 John 1:9).

Yes, we have a stockpile we must clean up, but God has an even larger "stockpile of forgiveness" ready to wash over us. The powerful blood of Christ can and will wash away our wrongs with one massive tidal wave of cleansing love.

From personal experience I can reassure you that—no matter what mountain of old trash you're facing—with God's help, your stockpile will be no problem. Trust Him. He stands ready to strengthen you until there isn't even one single sin left uncleansed, even in the darkest corner of your heart.

Step 3: Prepare Yourself for Doubts and Attacks

Now, watch out! As soon as change is about to happen, the enemies of progress—those looming obstacles—close in. Your comfortable old habits are one enemy. And Satan is another. He'll barrage you with doubts about whether you actually can or want to pull this thing off. An inner voice will protest: *I can't do this…it will never work…it's too hard…there are too many sins…other practical matters are a lot more pressing….* Anticipate this volley of doubt darts. Expect slipping confidence, backward glances, even despair. But remember that breaking through these attacks is the only route to higher ground.

Shrinking back now will only get you more of what you've tried and don't want.

I know all about this terrain. I've stumbled in fright and been pulled away by distraction. That's why I want to encourage you on. Shrinking back now will only get you more of what you've tried and don't want: more sin, failure, disobedience, and imprisonment; less of the incredible best that God holds out for you.

Rise up in faith, believe in the shed blood of Jesus the Savior, and walk straight on. You'll immediately discover that this attack lasts only as long as you permit it to.

Step 4: Ask the Lord to Reveal to You Everything in the Stockpile

Now you're ready for that all-important step: ask God to show you the whole truth.

Get in a quiet place, away from all distractions, including people and the phone. Make sure that you have at least an hour of uninterrupted time. Find a private place in your home, sit in a pew in your local church, or drive to a quiet spot in nature. Bring your Bible, a pad of paper, a pen...and some matches.

When you're settled, ask God to help you see your stockpile. The Lord wants your stockpile cleansed much more than you do. He will strengthen you in the process and reveal to you everything that needs to be dealt with. Pray out loud, pray slowly, pray from your heart, using some words like these:

> *Dear Lord,*
> *I humble myself before Your holiness.*
> *I enter Your courts and ask for Your grace and mercy.*
> *I am in a time of real need; I plead for Your help. Please help me!*
> *I want to obey Your command to cleanse myself of all sin.*
> *I want to become holy as You are holy in all of my conduct.*
> *I want to please You and make a new start in my life.*
> *Would You please reveal to me every sin in my stockpile?*
> *Show me what You see hidden in my heart.*
> *Bring to my memory, Holy Spirit,*
> *everything that grieves You.*
> *I hereby promise that, with Your help,*
> *I will do my part to cleanse every one.*
> *In Jesus' name, Amen.*

When you've finished praying, start writing. List on your pad every sin the Lord reveals, writing each one on a separate line. Don't evaluate, don't defend, don't wonder if you've already dealt with that sin. You don't even need to worry that someone else might read those awful words. Remember, you brought matches! No matter how painful or tentative the sin, no matter how big or little, long ago or recent, just record what the Holy Spirit brings into your thoughts.

To be thorough, I recommend praying through ten questions based on Paul's inventory of the "acts of the sinful nature" in Galatians 5:19–21. Pray each request slowly and out loud to the Lord, then pause quietly for a few seconds and write down any additional sins.

1. "Lord, who do I need to forgive who has hurt me?" Pause and write.
2. "Who have I hurt?" Pause and write.
3. "Have I ever stolen anything from anyone?" Pause and write.
4. "Have I ever lied or purposefully misled anyone?" Pause and write.
5. "Have I ever purposefully gossiped about anyone?" Pause and write.
6. "Bring to my mind all sexual sins." Pause and write.
7. "Do I have envy or hatred in my heart?" Pause and write.
8. "Have I sinned with drugs, alcohol, or wild parties?" Pause and write.
9. "In your sight, have I sinned in anger and wrath?" Pause and write.
10. "Do I have selfish ambition, or am I divisive?" Pause and write.

By this time, you're probably emotionally wrung out. That's to be expected—after all, the Lord is taking you through spiritual heart surgery, and being "broken" is part of the process. I remember the first time that I did The List years ago. It was one of the most discouraging days of my life. I could hardly believe what I read, but there it was in front of me in my own handwriting.

Your list is not who you are now; it is an honest accounting of what you did in the past.

Take heart. Your list is not who you are now; it is an honest accounting of what you did in the past. It is proof that you have completed a courageous step—looked backward to face the truth so you can turn forward and face the Lord with joy!

Step 5: Confess to the Lord Each Sin in the Stockpile One at a Time

Each sin we commit is an actual objective entity that is known by the Lord and is now, we trust, known by us. Each one is different, and each one has its own reality, including its consequence in our life. The Bible teaches that only once are all your sins forgiven *as a group*—at the point of salvation. From that point on, each is treated individually. Therefore, the Lord waits for us to confess each of our sins to Him. Through this process of confession, we'll experience His full forgiveness.

You might proceed now with your confession like this:

1. Kneel before the Lord—literally get on your knees. You've got some heavy apologies to offer to the Lord. Humble yourself. If that seems too difficult at this point, you'd better not move forward; your heart is still too stubborn.
2. Tell the Lord exactly what you are feeling at this point and why you are kneeling in His presence.
3. Work your way down the list, sin by sin, saying out loud something like this: "Lord, I confess to you that I sinned by_____. Forgive me and cleanse me from this unrighteousness."
4. Pray over each one slowly, from your heart. If one is difficult, circle it, and pray it over a second time before moving on to the next.
5. When you are done with your list, rest for a moment.
6. For those sins that seem especially pressing or difficult, confess them a third time. If something deeper still seems to remain, ask the Lord to help you. He will.

7. When you are done, pause and say to the Lord, "Is there anything else between us that I need to confess and deal with?" If anything else surfaces, write it on your pad and confess it.

Step 6: Restore Anything Affected by Your Sin Stockpile

I imagine that as you've proceeded through this time of confession, certain sins have "called out to you." They may need more than your confession—they may need acts of restoration.

Is there a blocked or soured relationship that you need to make right? Should you return something you stole? A deception you can now address truthfully? Don't delay in following through on whatever the Lord put on your heart. You've begun this remarkable cleansing; now complete it to consolidate your gains and keep God's power and favor flowing in your life.

I love to hear the victory and freedom stories from those who choose to restore: some have led enemies or estranged family members to the Lord just by humbling themselves and asking for forgiveness; some have contacted those they were previously immoral with to seek forgiveness and healing; many have forgiven those who wounded them, including those who have already died. One man told me he returned fifty cents stolen fifty years ago from the corner drugstore! Just think about that—for fifty years a foolish act had tainted his heart and conscience.

The final part of the restoration step is linked to sins that are still present in your life. You see, confession just won't work if down deep in your heart you are still intending to give in to some of those sins when you face temptation in the future. At this point, you must make a most important decision—to repent and turn from your sins and walk in obedience to the Lord.

At times, this means you must look squarely at your sins and get at the source of the temptation. I know many men and women who have canceled their cable and satellite contracts because they were watching pornography. Others emptied their liquor cabinet. Still others had to reject immorality by ending a sexually impure relationship.

Whatever beast you may face, be assured that the Lord will help you conquer it through His grace. If you find yourself falling back into sin, share it with a trusted, older believer of the same gender (see James 5). Ask the person to hold you accountable until you establish a pattern of victory. If you would like more help breaking free from a stronghold in your life, I recommend that you read my book *Personal Holiness in Times of Temptation,* especially beginning on page 110, where I present the "Ten Step Deep Cleanse."

Finally, look at the hardest situations you face and ask the Lord, "What do you want me to do to bring my life into obedience and be free of sin?" Whatever you do, don't start with the easy sins, because you'll never finish. You'll soon be compromised and defeated again. Instead, immediately deal with the single toughest problem and see it through to completion.

In spite of the pain, you'll be lifted up by God's joy and strength—because you're being set free by obedience to His will.

Step 7: Burn Your Old Stock List and Celebrate Your Cleansing

It may take you a day, or a few days, or even a week or two at the most, but you are eventually going to finish your list—and your conscience will be fully clean before God and man. In the years ahead, you are going to realize that this major act of "cleansing yourself" will turn out to be one of the most important milestones in your life.

When you are done, reach for that match.

At an appropriate and safe place, take your list and burn it, all the while thanking Jesus for His death on the cross and His unfailing forgiveness. As the last paper is turned to ashes, rejoice that each of those sins is out of your heart.

When a sin becomes no longer acceptable to you, you have a breakthrough with God.

If the enemy brings them back to accuse and defeat you, you must not stand for it for even a single moment. Just say out loud, "I have fully confessed the sin of _____ and hereby declare the truth that I am fully forgiven and under the precious blood of Jesus."

Celebrate, my friend. You have experienced a spiritual breakthrough of immense proportions.

A LAST WORD ABOUT THAT GARAGE OF MINE

God used a donkey to get Balaam's attention. Out of the mouth of that lowly beast came a message that this supposedly smart man couldn't seem to receive any other way. That garage of mine taught me something, too: When a sin becomes no longer acceptable to you, you have a breakthrough with God.

I remember the sense of complete orderliness, cleanliness, and openness as I stood there in the middle of the garage. Not only did I discover incredible freedom—and a few things that had been missing for months—but the communication between me and my wife improved dramatically. Somehow, coming to the end of that stockpile inspired me. In fact, I marched right into the house and went to war on my closet.

There's one thing I've noticed, though, about clean garages and clean hearts. The best way to stay clean is make *clean* a way of life.

How do we accomplish that in our spiritual lives? Surely you've asked this question often. Every serious disciple longs to sin less, to make progress in understanding the root causes of sin in our lives, to honor the Lord with a steadily improving record of resisting temptation.

In the next chapter, I want to help you take a look at the very core of your being, the inner chambers of your motivations and needs. It's the place where most of those stupid mistakes and stubborn rebellions start. And God has a breakthrough waiting for you there, too.

Chapter Six

Habits of Deception

BREAKING THROUGH TO FREEDOM

*T*hese days I rarely get around to reading the funny papers. (Is that still what they call them?) But some years ago I came across a Calvin and Hobbes cartoon strip that has always stuck with me.

It went like this: Calvin's red wagon is racing along under a blue sky thanks to Hobbes the tiger, his imaginary friend, who is pushing from behind.

"It's true, Hobbes," the boy says, "ignorance *is* bliss!" Calvin steers straight toward a dark forest. "Once you know things, you start seeing problems everywhere, and once you see problems, you feel like you ought to try to fix them, and…."

The cartoon duo is now whizzing down a narrow path between trees. Hobbes has jumped on board. Calvin steers the wagon into the curves like Mario Andretti. "And fixing problems always seems to require a personal change," he shouts over his shoulder, "and change means doing things that aren't fun! I say phooey to that!"

Hobbes's striped head barely misses a branch. Good thing that Calvin can steer without looking. Then suddenly the wagon clears the forest and shoots over the crest of a hill. Along with the wagon, Calvin's speech gathers speed. "But if you're willfully stupid, you don't know any better, so you can keep doing whatever you like!" he yells. "The secret to happiness is short-term, stupid self-interest!"

The red wagon careens into an empty white frame on the page. Hobbes's eyes pop. "We're heading for that cliff!" he screams.

But Calvin covers his eyes. "I don't want to know about it," he says.

Next, a frame of blue sky. Across the middle of it, red wagon, imaginary tiger, and blond boy sail separately into nothing but space— "Waaauggghhhhh!"

Last frame. Hobbes is a very flat tiger with stars swirling around his head. "I'm not sure I can stand so much bliss," he says into the dirt.

From near his bent-up wagon, Calvin replies, "Careful! We don't want to learn anything from this."

I love that cartoon strip. For one thing, I've been in that red wagon a few times myself, spouting the same kind of easy rhetoric. Who among us hasn't felt that same lust for a thrill, the dizzying appeal of foolish behaviors, the reluctance to reach for personal change. And not surprisingly, our lives end up in that same disappointing heap.

We're complicated, conflicted beings who want more than one thing at a time. Mostly, we want to feel better now.

Calvin, the cartoon theologian, introduces our topic for this chapter: "short-term, stupid self-interest."

God's word for it is sin.

In the previous chapter we talked about cleaning out the pile of sin in our lives. Now we are ready to learn how to keep the garage from filling up again. I want to help you look under the surface of your life, peel back the layers, and ask hard questions: "Why do I sin repeatedly in certain areas?" "How can I say that I love God and want to know Him better, please Him more, and become more like Him—and still fall into sin on a regular basis?"

What is the real reason so many well-intentioned Christians race down the hill of temptation, sail off the cliff of sin, and land in a heap of ruin?

We all have our little red wagons, our trusty collection of rationalizations, and our fat scrapbook of resulting disasters. But we live like this for reasons, however hidden they might be to us. We're complicated, conflicted beings who want more than one thing at a time. Mostly, we want to feel better now.

Somehow Satan uses all this expertly against us, doesn't he? He hopes the day will never come that we choose to take our hands away from our eyes and learn something. Satan knows too, I believe, that you and I can't make our next spiritual breakthrough without doing exactly that. We'll never break free of the sin cycle in our lives until we take steps to deal with the persistent appeal of sin itself.

I'll admit that this is dark and intimidating terrain. You may not even feel ready to consider taking this step toward maturity. But if you are willing to press on, be assured that God will receive your efforts as an act of worship, not just as an admission of failure.

And as you read, remember that:

- to talk about sin doesn't make us sinful;
- to confess to the presence of recurring sin in our lives doesn't mean we're not saved; and
- to admit to the pull of sin doesn't relegate us to the broken parts bin of God's family.

None other than the apostle Paul wrote: "For what I am doing, I do not understand. For what I will to do that I do not practice; but what I hate, that I do.... O wretched man that I am! Who will deliver me...?" (Romans 7:15, 24). The struggle against sin for this giant of the faith was very real. But unlike comic-book Calvin, Paul had thrown off ignorance as an excuse. He was pressing toward a breakthrough with every confidence, crying out to his Lord for the truth, for help, and for grace.

That's what we will do together now.

YOUR PERSONAL SIN PROFILE

When I lead conference groups to experience spiritual breakthroughs in this area, I ask participants to make an inventory of the recurring one or two sins that trouble them most. Call it a Personal Sin Profile if you will. The questions go something like this:

1. What day of the week do you sin the most?
2. What time of the day do you sin the most?
3. Where are you when you sin the most?
4. Who is with you when you sin the most?
5. What is the sin you commit the most in these circumstances?
6. What are the specific emotions you feel right before you sin?

To drive the point of question 6 home, I then ask them to turn their answer into a personal finding: "The emotions that I feel right before I give in to temptation are _____."

Conferees are usually startled to discover that *those feelings are always the same ones.* Each time they are tempted to sin, regardless of the sin, the feelings preceding their choice don't vary, just the circumstances.

Then I ask them to take what they've learned one step further—question 7: "At that point, what does every temptation you face promise you?"

By now, you probably know their reply: "The promise is that if I commit that sin, the negative feeling I'm experiencing at the time will go away or be replaced by a positive feeling I like."

At this point, I ask the conferees to write down all the words that best describe what they are usually feeling right before they sin. Can you anticipate their choices? Take a moment to ask yourself the same question.

If your answers are like everyone else's, you'll have written down words like overwhelmed, lonely, alienated, rejected, unhappy, bored, betrayed, useless, "in gnawing pain over something I can't put my finger on," discontented, a failure, frightened, and anxious.

Obviously, what the temptation offers—actually seems to promise— is exactly the opposite of those negative feelings. Instead of all those powerful negative emotions, the sin offers soothing, positive ones. Or, as I've come to believe, a sense of comfort.

Two dominant motives lie at the root of why we sin.

Reason 1: We seek the pleasure that comes from that sin.

Reason 2: We seek the absence of pain that is the immediate source of our temptation to commit that sin.

Sound the same? In important ways, they're not. Take the issue of drunkenness. Ultimately, people get drunk for one of two reasons: First, they like the initial sense of euphoria and personal liberty that they initially feel when they are under the influence of alcohol. Going out with the guys on Friday night, for instance, is usually for the purpose of having a good time. Drunkenness is for fun.

If, however, drunkenness occurs in the privacy of one's home or office and occurs on a regular basis, then more likely the reason for the alcohol isn't for fun. Instead, the motive now is to dull some inner pain that just won't go away. The sin of drunkenness at this point, then, is motivated not by the promise of pleasure but by the motive to get rid of that pain.

We could see sexual immorality in the same light. Sex is pleasurable, but many use it more like a drug—to mask the pain of loneliness, alienation, or feelings of powerlessness.

Is looking for a presence of pleasure wrong in God's sight? Is looking for an absence of pain wrong in God's sight?

Absolutely not. In fact, the Lord made us all the same in this matter: None of us like pain, and all of us like pleasure. *The issue isn't the motive, it's the method.* It's looking for the right thing in the wrong place. But once you understand the two reasons for sin—sin for pleasure, sin for relief of pain—several important spiritual breakthroughs are at hand.

The breakthroughs I want to focus on here begin with questions:

If you drink for pleasure, wouldn't you be less likely to get drunk if you found yourself feeling comforted? If you drink to mask pain, wouldn't you stop drinking to excess if the pain were gone?

REACHING FOR COMFORT

Years ago, I made a dramatic breakthrough in my understanding of sin. In a particular area of my life, I so wanted not to sin, but I found myself at times seemingly overwhelmed by temptation. Was there no real answer for victory, I wondered? I still remember exactly where I was sitting when the Lord opened my understanding to an obvious, but little understood, answer that has helped me and thousands of others.

Here's what happened: When I discovered that my emotions right before every temptation were distressed to some level and I was actually seeking comfort, I asked God to show me another way to find it. That's when I remembered the promise of Jesus to send someone to be my personal comforter! Listen to what he told his disciples in the upper room:

> *I discovered that my emotions right before every temptation were distressed.*
>
>

And I will pray the Father, and he shall give you another Comforter, that he may abide with you for ever; Even the Spirit of truth; whom the world cannot receive, because it seeth him not, neither knoweth him: but ye known him, for he dwelleth with you, and shall be in you. (John 14:16–17, KJV)

Incredibly, Jesus gave us the Holy Spirit to be "in" us and to be our ever-present personal source of comfort. Somehow, I'd never linked this provision to my struggle with sin. As these thoughts rushed through my mind, I wondered what would happen if I specifically asked for this comfort in a time of temptation. Would the Holy Spirit give to me the desperately needed comfort so that I would feel less need to sin?

I decided to try. My simple request went like this: "Dear Holy Spirit, You've been sent to me to be my personal Comforter. I am in desperate need of comfort. I don't want to sin. Please comfort me. In Jesus' name, Amen."

That was it. I took off my watch to see what would happen and when.

At first, absolutely nothing did. How discouraged and defeated I felt at that moment. But then I slowly became aware of something—I felt comforted! I didn't know exactly when I was comforted, I only knew that I was—and that my soul felt soothed and no longer in pain.

When I turned back toward that temptation, I discovered that it had miraculously slithered back into the darkness, far away from my senses. I was free. Instead of finding it hard not to sin at that moment, I found it easy because the need to sin had faded, and my heart was surrounded with satisfaction and warmth.

I've prayed to my Comforter many times since that first occasion, and I've discovered two immutable truths: the Holy Spirit always—and I mean always—completes His responsibility in my heart; and He always gives me His comfort within three minutes, though I can never put my finger on the moment when He does.

Now I call this prayer for comfort the "Three-Minute Temptation Buster." The next time you feel tempted to sin, realize that you are also feeling negative emotions and your heart has a void and needs comfort. Take that deep need to God. Ask for his Comforter to come to you. Then take off your watch and time yourself—I can guarantee that the Spirit will comfort you in less than three minutes. And then you won't need to sin because the temptation no longer exists.

GETTING TO THE SOURCE

There's a second answer to dealing with the kind of inner pain that sends us in search of relief. It lies not in finding comfort for the pain, but in trying to remove the pain at its source.

Every pain or negative emotion becomes fertile ground for temptation, and unless they are physically related, each one is rooted in an unresolved issue or event in our lives. As part of your journey of spiritual breakthroughs, I encourage you to begin asking God to reveal to you the cause of your inner distress. I promise you He will. Based on my experience and that of many others, I've found that an astounding 70 percent of our inner pain is rooted in unforgiveness; 20 percent seems to stem from unresolved personal conflicts; and everything else accounts for the remaining 10 percent.

As we saw in the last chapter, by dealing with your unforgiveness and your unresolved personal conflicts, your pain will seem to disappear into thin air. Consequently, your temptations will rapidly diminish, too, losing much of their power and frequency. And you will experience the nearness of God like never before. Why? Because when you're trapped in sin, guilt and shame raise a spiritual barrier in your heart that leaves you feeling that God is a million miles away. He's really not, of course; He is just on the other side of this breakthrough, ready to comfort you, lead you through the steps of forgiveness and reconciliation, and help you through any other difficult situation.

In chapters 5 and 12 the steps of confession, cleansing, and restoration for deep-seated issues of bitterness and unforgiveness are carefully presented. Read those chapters prayerfully and courageously. Remember, you are never alone as you press toward a deeper commitment to holiness in your life. God cares about these hidden, painful experiences that haunt your life and trip you up on your spiritual journey.

Have you really grasped how much God *wants* to bring satisfaction, healing, and comfort into your life? Here are some key passages for you to meditate on and remember in your struggle with sin:

And my God shall supply all you need according to His riches in
glory by Christ Jesus. (Philippians 4:19)

Peace I leave with you. My peace I give to you; not as the world
gives do I give to you. Let not your heart be troubled, neither let
it be afraid. (John 14:27)

You will show me the path of life; In Your presence is fullness of
joy; At Your right hand are pleasures forevermore. (Psalm 16:11)

These verses remind us that God wants to supply our needs and grant
us His wonderful inner peace as we follow Him in complete obedience. The
most satisfied person in all the world is the First Chair person who walks by
means of the Holy Spirit and who has faced the failures and wounds of the
past and worked through each of them until they have been fully resolved.

AT THE CORE OF YOUR BEING

We've looked briefly at how pain in our emotions and circumstances
can motivate us to seek relief through sin. Now it's time to go still deeper—
right to that dark, mysterious center of your being that only God can
see completely.

At the core, pain and dissatisfaction arise in different ways than
from distress over circumstances, broken relationships, or unmet
physical and emotional needs. Often, they *feel* the same to us, and we
try to alleviate them in the same ways. But they're different. One is
rooted in circumstances and in our physical natures; the other in our
spiritual nature.

Let me explain. In the beginning, God created Adam and Eve in His
image and made a world for them where they had personal fellowship
and union with the Lord *every day, every moment.* But since the Fall, we've
experienced an unrelieved hunger for His person and presence. Because
God designed us spiritual beings, we have a nagging awareness that life is
far beyond what we can see, hear, and touch.

This void, or driving need, is one that every human feels. It was intended by God to drive us to seek Him. Think of this emptiness at the core as a vacuum ever seeking to be filled, as a homesickness that we, as God's children, have to be with him, to experience him more fully, and one day, to be reunited with him in heaven.

God's intention for this hunger for Him is that we will satisfy it with Him. But humans deal with the void in many ways. (Just because it is spiritual in nature doesn't mean that people bring spiritual priorities to the task.) For example, busyness must be one of the most common responses. Busyness hides the reality of the emptiness for a while. Television, sports, and music are all used to plug up the emptiness. The pull of the void, however, is relentless. And God's greatest favor may be that He never releases us from the pull in our souls that says, "Come, my child, find Me!"

Listen to the apostle Paul talk about this void in his speech to the Athenians:

> *This void was intended by God to drive us to seek Him.*
>
>

And He [God] has made from one blood [Adam and Eve] every nation of men to dwell on all the face of the earth, and has determined their preappointed times and the boundaries of their habitation, so that they should seek the Lord, in the hope that they might grope for Him and find Him, though He is not far from each one of us; for in Him we live and move and have our being.... "For we are also His offspring." (Acts 17:26–28)

Did you catch that word, "grope," for Him? Even though God is not far from us, we must choose to reach for Him. As you can imagine, how we respond to this inner void, and what we reach for to fill it, has everything to do with which Chair of commitment we're sitting in.

The First Chair Christian relishes this void as the stimulus for all that becomes the most meaningful in his life. This person has discovered that an intimate relationship with the Lord satisfies the void. In fact, the void reverses, becoming instead a river of life and blessing flowing out of his or her being (John 7:37–39). The psalms are full of testimonies of how First Chair believers have directed their innermost hungers toward the God who satisfies (see especially Psalms 23, 42, and 119).

The Second Chair Christian admits the void but doesn't trust that God alone can fill it. The moment this person became a Christian, the Holy Spirit entered his heart and began whispering the profound possibilities for an unbroken relationship with Him. But although there have been seasons of First Chair fellowship, they have been shallow or short-lived. Yet the Second Chair person is certain that he or she is getting the best of both worlds—a little of God, a little of the world. After all, God can't be trusted with too much control. (Isn't He a kill-joy and fun-hater anyway?) For all but the spiritually gifted, like saints and preachers, selling out to God can wait until heaven. In the here and now, a Chair Two Christian crams the void with possessions, career, sex, recreation, and judicious doses of religion. At least he or she knows that their eternal salvation is in the bag.

The Third Chair person senses the void but—since a personal relationship with God seems out of the question—tries to fill it with substitutes: spirituality, false religion, art, music, or passionate pursuits of various kinds. These substitutes are idols—reinvented gods created from a person's own thoughts, feelings, values, and imagination. The person in Chair Three may conclude that the void is a weakness of temperament, a tendency to melancholy, rather than the created incompleteness of man. Popular songs, novels, and movies are full of stories about the void: how, for example, a love relationship can save you from it, or how nothing can, and since that's all there is, you might as well eat, drink, and be merry.

Where are you and I in this picture right now? I'm sure you understand what's at stake: if we don't face the truth about our natures, the void which can pull us toward God will be used by Satan to drag us into sin again and again.

POOR MAN IN THE PALACE

All this raises a key question: If the hole in our centers is God-shaped, as Augustine said, why would nearly everyone—well-meaning Christians included—try to fill it with anything else?

I believe one reason is that we don't always believe God is telling us the truth. Specifically, we doubt that it's possible to really connect with God in an ongoing, intimate, satisfying relationship. This is Second Chair thinking, of course. As a result, we respond foolishly to the pain in our second layer (motivations, needs, wants) and the emptiness in our inner core (our God-shaped spiritual void).

In fact, we can get so good at filling the void in our heart with substitutes for God's presence that we hardly notice the ache anymore. Amazingly enough, we fail to see how consistently our own attempts to fill those needs lead us into sin and misery. Like Calvin, even when we crash, we'd rather not learn something that might threaten our control of our own lives.

We can get so good at filling the void in our heart with substitutes for God's presence that we hardly notice the ache anymore.

Jesus says that at those moments when we think we're in control, we're not; when we're serving our own best interests, we're betraying our destinies; when we think we're getting the best deal possible by holding out on God, we're actually living like paupers.

Remember Jesus' impassioned message to the Christians in Laodicea:

Because you say "I am rich, have become wealthy, and have need of nothing"—and do not know that you are wretched, miserable, poor, blind, and naked—I counsel you to buy from Me gold refined in the fire, that you may be rich; and white garments, that you may be clothed, that the shame of your nakedness may not be revealed; and anoint your eyes with eye salve, that you may see." (Revelation 3:17–18)

Here we have the top-down perspective on our little wagon ride down the hill. What seems to be self-interest turns out to be loss. The man who seems to have it all (the compromised Christian) turns out to be the poor man in the palace.

Now look at Jesus' familiar, comforting invitation to each of us, His willful, straying children: "Behold, I stand at the door and knock. If anyone hears My voice and opens the door, I will come in to him and dine with him, and he with Me" (Revelation 3:20).

We could paraphrase Jesus' message: "Yes, I am here to save you and take you to heaven when you die. But so much more is possible *right now* if you'll let me in."

And look at how Jesus describes that void in the center, that empty room of longing for something more—a banqueting room of fellowship, plenty, and ultimate satisfaction!

Although Jesus always takes the first step in coming toward the person (by His constant knocking), He always waits for our decision to invite Him further and deeper into our lives (by opening the door to that room in our heart).

Jesus then assures the lukewarm Christian that if invited, He will respond—He will "dine with him." In the culture of that time, to dine with another person meant to establish a close and meaningful relationship. The one who opened up the door to another invited him or her to a friendship. And this relationship will be two-sided: "I will dine with him, and he [will dine] with Me."

Take an inventory of what you've put in that empty room at the center. Have you filled that void with other things so that dining intimately with Christ would be awkward or impossible?

The first breakthrough invitation, then, from this truth about your core is to firmly, persistently, and prayerfully set aside every other method of filling the God-void except with God Himself. When you do so, you will begin to hunger even more for Him—and that very hunger will draw you toward the spiritual growth and vigor you long for.

Leaf through David's spiritual journal, where he records in the book of Psalms how he let the hunger at his core push him away from sin and toward God:

> When You said, "Seek My face,"
> My heart said to You, "Your face, Lord, I will seek."
> (Psalm 27:8)

> The young lions lack and suffer hunger;
> But those who seek the Lord shall not lack any good thing.
> (Psalm 34:10)

> As the deer pants for the water brooks,
> So pants my soul for You, O God.
> (Psalm 42:1)

> You will show me the path of life;
> In Your presence is fullness of joy;
> At Your right hand are pleasures forevermore.
> (Psalm 16:11)

LEANING TOWARD GOD

Once you have emptied your core of all the competing substitutes, you're ready to make a second breakthrough. This happens when you incline your heart toward God. Joshua understood this when he instructed the nation of Israel after they had once again chosen the Lord:

You are witnesses…that you have chosen the Lord…to serve Him…. Now therefore…put away the foreign gods which are among you, and incline your heart to the Lord God of Israel. (Joshua 24:22–23)

Choosing the Lord is not the same as inclining your heart to the Lord. Serving the Lord is not the same as inclining your heart to the Lord. Putting away sin and false worship isn't the same as inclining your heart to the Lord. Inclining your heart to the Lord means to redirect all your heart's longings toward Him and only Him.

Picture a plant that leans with every fiber of its being toward the ray of light that comes through the window each morning. David not only longed for God this way but determined to direct all the passions and plans of his heart toward God's will, not his. Listen as he encourages his son, Solomon, to seek this kind of relationship with the Lord:

As for you, my son Solomon, know the God of your father, and serve Him with a loyal heart and with a willing mind; for the Lord searches all hearts and understands all the intent of the thoughts. If you seek Him, He will be found by you. (1 Chronicles 28:9)

> *Picture a plant that leans with every fiber of its being toward the ray of light that comes through the window each morning.*
>
>

Friend, no matter how deeply you feel that hunger at your core, I can promise you that God is not trying to hide Himself from you! When you choose to seek Him, you will find Him. He is using your surrendered longing for Him to draw you further into the center of His best for you. Just like in the Garden of Eden, the Lord God wants to return and walk in the coolness of the morning with you.

To extend yourself in search of God usually comes down to a few very practical decisions. Does it mean you choose to rise earlier each day to seek Him in His Word? Does it mean you jealously guard the quiet moments of the day to simply listen for the sound of His voice? Does it mean you need to notice what priorities start to incline your heart toward other uses for your time and energy?

Whatever choices face you, take action today. God is ready to enter and minister to your innermost longings if you lean toward Him and His goodness with all your might.

HURTLING TOWARD HOME

We've covered a lot of ground since we first went hurtling down that slope with Calvin and Hobbes. And since we are determined to actually learn something—let's do the unthinkable: a quick review. In fact, this is such a critical chapter that I recommend you do what might be unthinkable to Calvin and go back and read it again to make sure you didn't miss anything.

We started out with the question, "Is it really possible to sin less, to keep that garage from filling up again?"

I promised you that the answer was yes. But the key to overcoming sin was to understand more about what drives us to sin. We learned that we experience two main urges that drive us to sin: to feel pleasure or to avoid pain. We discovered two breakthrough ways to deal with these urges:

1. We can go to God to find comfort.

2. We can deal positively with the source of our pain.

Then we moved deeper. We learned that our hunger for God originates from a spiritual emptiness or void we experience at the core of our being. This void can cause us to sin if we seek false ways to fill it. But we arrived at two breakthrough ways God invites us to respond to this mysterious and powerful urge:

1. We need to discover and evict any substitutes we've relied on to fill our God-void and let that void draw us toward God alone.

2. We need to incline our hearts—lean with all our most fundamental passions and affections—toward God.

With God's grace and power, you are well on your way to experiencing a lifestyle of victory over sin. You see, a stockpile of sin is optional. Spiritual defeat is never inevitable. The next time your wagon is racing toward a cliff, you'll know that God cares about why you do what you do. My prayer is that God will use these truths in your life to turn you away from another crash and bring you hurtling toward home instead.

What a relief it is for seeking Christians to know that living in the grip of "short-term, stupid self-interest" is just not what God has in mind for any one of us. It's not only possible but entirely within our inheritance to walk daily in a satisfying, comforting, and healing relationship with our Creator God.

And—too bad Calvin didn't learn this—that's exactly as much bliss as any human can stand.

Experiencing Breakthroughs in Your Marriage

Chapter Seven

The Key to Her Heart

Breaking through to Love and Leadership

A friend of mine whose marriage is an inspiration to me called not too long ago. "Hey, Bruce, I've got a question," he said. He sounded confused.

"Sure, go ahead, Dan," I replied. "You okay?"

"Well, I guess so. I was wondering if we're really strange?" Then he laughed, but I could tell he had something on his mind. "Bruce, is a terrific marriage really *supposed* to be normal? Or am I an alien?"

Was that ever a setup for a wisecrack, but I let my friend continue. He told me he had just come back from a cross-country flight. During the trip he'd wandered to the back of the plane to get a Coke. He said he was happy and humming a tune. One of the flight attendants seemed curious.

"You sure are happy," she said to Dan.

"Well, yes, I am," he said.

She wanted to know why.

"Oh, that's easy. I'm celebrating my twenty-sixth wedding anniversary when I get home, and I can't wait to get there!"

Then Dan said to me, "Bruce, she looked at me like maybe I was lying through my teeth. Maybe had too many cocktails. She couldn't believe I had been married that long to one person and was still happy about it. I told her, 'Ma'am, I'm thrilled about it!'"

Dan asked her about her marriage. Turns out she had been married, but now was divorced. Somehow their little exchange got a conversation going in the back of the plane. Attendants and passengers started chipping in. The consensus of the women was that they had given up on marriage generally and finding a good man in particular.

Finally the first flight attendant said, "Sir, I don't know of a single person who is happily married."

"You've got to be kidding," Dan replied. "You don't know of anybody?"

"Nobody." Then Dan said she got a funny little smile on her face. "You don't have a brother who's single, do you?"

I told Dan he had something everybody wants.

After a pause, Dan said, "I guess I was flattered by the comment at the time. But the more I've thought about it, the more I wonder, *What's going on in our world? And what are we going to do about it?*

I don't know where your marriage is today, friend. If you ran into some disillusioned flight attendants, what would they see in your eye as you spoke of your marriage?

I wish I could tell you that if you're in Chair One in your walk with God, you'll automatically have a blissful marriage. But I can't. It's true that wholehearted spiritual commitments will affect every single area of your life for the better. But most of us still need to make solid and significant breakthroughs in the critical areas of our day-to-day lives.

That includes our marriage. (Even though I'm speaking directly to husbands in this chapter, and wives in the next, I encourage wives to read along here. Knowing what God expects of your husband can only help you to help him.)

If you're a husband whose marriage is stuck in Chair Two—limping along, injured, in some respects dishonoring to both God and your spouse—this chapter is for you. If you've yet to be married, or your marriage is thriving in Chair One, this chapter is *still* for you—as the message may help you avoid some all-too-common pitfalls most marriages encounter sooner or later.

BACK TO THE BASICS

Most of the time if something's not working in our marriage, we need to go back to the basics. When your home computer doesn't come on, you don't haul the whole setup out to the trash. You check the power cord, the connections, how you're using the disks. You reach for the manual.

Creating a First Chair marriage begins with a willingness to reexamine fundamental questions about how you relate to your wife (just as First Chair faith began with reexamining how you relate to God). In the same way you would reach for your computer user's manual, I ask you to trust in and reach for God's revealed plan in the Bible.

In fact, you may have heard before what I have to share with you. (More likely, it floated by your ears at a time when you were less motivated, and now you're tempted to think you've "heard it before.") Or you might be thinking, "Oh, marriage—well, mine is pretty much what it is and what it's always going to be." Or "But you haven't met *my* wife!"

Listen, if you're willing to humble yourself in God's presence as you read these pages, the Holy Spirit will show you new, life-changing opportunities. And they may be right where you thought only ho-hum words existed—I've seen it happen hundreds of times.

First, take a moment to consider how a husband is usually depicted in the media: He's forever at the office or bar, flirtatious, unfaithful, driven by money or power, a complete dunce around the kids, untrustworthy, interested in sex more than his next breath, and prone to fistfights when drunk.

But of course he drives a nice car and has a washboard stomach.

Now consider the promise of a First Chair Christian marriage:

The promise of a First Chair marriage is that you will experience deeply fulfilling friendship, affection, and sex; you will build together a loving home and a family of godly children; and you will receive from your wife the kind of respect and support you need to accomplish your special mission on earth.

You can see why it's not an overstatement to say that a godly—read that, "God-designed"—marriage is actually what every sensible husband wants. Why try on some other kind of male-female relationship that we were never created for? Why settle for a TV version, no matter how glitzy? We will only end up in disappointment and failure.

Let me ask you to do a few things as you read the rest of this chapter. Leave aside all those false messages that pollute our understanding and expectations. Put your pride in a brown bag and drop-kick it out into the alley. Think carefully and wisely through the biblical job description for a husband. Be willing to make critical, possibly painful, decisions and follow through.

A godly—read that, "God-designed"— marriage is actually what every sensible husband wants.

And—here's the best part—expect a breakthrough in your marriage.

A HUSBAND'S ROLE

All of the deeply satisfied marriages that I'm familiar with have one thing in common: The spouses understand the biblical basis for their respective roles and responsibilities—and fulfill them even when the going gets tough.

Your *role* defines your purpose and overall objective. It's described by a job title. At work, your role might be manager, for example.

Your *responsibilities,* on the other hand, define how you carry out your job description. Managers are usually responsible for organizing and assisting people to get work done.

Setting aside all your preconceptions about the role of the husband, what one word would you choose to describe that role according to the Bible?

Read this verse to locate the one word that fits: "For the husband is head of the wife, as also Christ is head of the church; and He is the Savior of the body" (Ephesians 5:23).

The overarching role of the man in marriage is to be the head. He is to be the head in a similar way that Christ is head of the Church.

But how is Christ the head? Head means to be the one who is delegated the authority, the one who is responsible, the person in charge, the leader, the one who takes care of the needs of those beneath His headship.

Did you notice that the Bible doesn't say, "For the husband should *try* to be the head of the wife"? No, it says, "the husband *is* the head."

Which leads to a question you might be asking yourself right now: What are you supposed to do then if your wife is smarter than you by a long shot, loves to lead and take charge, and you don't? Why not put her as head of the family?

Because God never intended marriage roles to be decided like they are in the corporate world, where only competency counts. For reasons of His own, God fashioned the man to lead and the woman to respond to his leadership in marriage. And a Chair One marriage is a relationship where the Lord's plan reigns supreme. In case you're already shopping for a throne for you and a tea tray for your wife, wait up. You should know that this role of headship is strictly limited. The Bible teaches that the man has been given this role of authority in only two areas—in marriage and in the church.

Beyond being in charge in your marriage, as head you must make sure that the people you are responsible for are happy, content, well provided for, protected, and fulfilled. Consider your role model. Jesus gave Himself completely and sacrificially for the needs and interests of His bride, the church.

Let me assure you, any normal wife will delight to follow a man who always looks out for her interests, even when the going gets difficult.

If we look more closely at Paul's description of how Christ is the head of His church, we will see a three-point unfolding of what our roles as husbands should look like:

Husbands, love your wives, just as Christ also loved the church and gave Himself for it,

- that He might sanctify and cleanse it with the washing of water by the word,
- that He might present it to Himself a glorious church, not having spot or wrinkle or any such thing, but
- that it should be holy and without blemish.

So, husbands ought to love their own wives. (Ephesians 5:26–28)

There it is—Christ's "role" as head of His bride, the Church, is to bring her to wholeness, holiness, and beauty; in other words, to help her achieve the full measure of what God intends for her life.

> *You should be able to evaluate your effectiveness in the headship role by noticing its results in your wife.*
>
>

If you look past the religious language in this passage, you'll make some amazing discoveries for your own marriage. Notice, for example, that all of Christ's reasons for loving the church are concerned with what He can do for the church, not with what the church does for Him.

Hmmm. Suddenly, headship doesn't look quite so uppity. (You're thinking, *Maybe I should be buying that tea tray for me to serve her!*)

Let me take you one step further: If all this is true, you should be able to evaluate your effectiveness in the headship role by noticing its results in your wife.

I'll never forget Mrs. Tracey. She was the dean of women at the college Darlene and I attended in New Jersey. A dignified New Englander, she brought a lot of class to the college. One day, ten years after we graduated, I met Mrs. Tracey in the hall when I returned to campus for a visit. As we chatted about the past, a couple who had graduated twenty years earlier walked up and joined in the reminiscing.

At one point in the conversation, Mrs. Tracey exclaimed to the wife, "Why, you are just radiant! You have a marvelous glow about you. Really, you're much more beautiful now than you were as a student years ago!"

Then, with hardly a pause, she gave the husband an approving look and said, "And you, young man. As her husband, you did that!"

For days I thought about Mrs. Tracey's profound double compliment. Could a husband take that kind of credit? Really be that influential simply by being the head God intended him to be?

The next time I looked at Paul's marriage teachings in Ephesians, they nearly leaped off the page. Of course Mrs. Tracey was right. She had simply recognized the pattern of Jesus' headship in a husband by looking at the face of his beautiful wife. And she was only pointing out in one godly marriage what God offers and expects from us all.

Take a minute to ask yourself: If I looked into my wife's eyes, if I watched her life for a week, could read her thoughts, feel her emotions, sense her soul—what would I discover about my headship?

CORRECTING YOUR SWING

By this time you might be saying, "Easy to imagine, a little tougher to pull off." So I want to help you think through any hindrances that might be keeping you from this powerful role of biblical headship in your marriage.

Marriage counselors and wives tend to agree on at least one "headship hindrance": Too many husbands tip like a sandman in one direction or the other, either too aggressive or too passive.

Husbands who swing in the direction of aggression throw their weight around as if they are the center of the family solar system. "If I'm the boss, you must be the slave," these husbands declare. For them, headship means they finally have someone who is locked into serving their needs, responding to their every whim. But aggressors do more than just hold the reins of a family. They usually start yanking on them selfishly, heedless of how things might feel on the bridle end. And unfortunately, aggressors often end up as abusers, hurting the very ones they promised to love and protect.

If you swing at all in this direction, I have bad news—you're not much appreciated, admired, or respected by your wife or family. The more you dominate, the more you will live as a stranger in your own house, whether you're aware of it or not. And I guarantee you won't be getting what you really want out of your marriage either. In fact, you'll be trapped in a web of illusion. You've mistaken power for strength and control for unity.

What about husbands who swing in the direction of passivity? These men find it easier to let the wife carry the load of decision making. "She handles risks better," they conclude. Contrary to what you might think, an overly passive husband is not less selfish than an aggressor. He has just learned to get what he wants differently—by letting someone else take the heat while he takes it easy. The passive husbands I've met start out apathetic, then abdicate their leadership role, and sometimes abandon the relationship altogether.

If you swing anywhere in this direction, you face—believe it or not—virtually the same bad news as the aggressor. You're not much appreciated, admired, or respected by your wife or family. You live increasingly as a stranger in your own house, and you're not getting what you were created for in marriage. And you, too, have bought into some costly deceptions: you've mistaken detachment for peace and irresponsibility for blamelessness.

What is God's better plan for husbands?

I like to describe it as strength in balance. The balanced position is the one right in the middle of both of those unfortunate traits. With strength in balance, you are in a place to grow, flourish, and succeed. As you become an authentic, responsible, and caring leader in your marriage, you'll be enjoying the marriage you've always wanted—and the one that pleases God.

I'll be honest: Every husband I know struggles with how he should accomplish this. Often, he makes mistakes because he's patterning himself after the wrong examples. Perhaps he tries to husband like some boss he used to work for. Perhaps he tries to parent his wife as if she were a child.

In a conversation with his friends, Jesus explained how His disciples could learn from, not emulate, the bad bosses of their day.

But Jesus called them to Himself and said to them, "You know that those who are considered rulers over the Gentiles lord it over them, and their great ones exercise authority over them. Yet it shall not be so among you." (Mark 10:42–43)

The more you dominate, the more you will live as a stranger in your own house.

Nestled in that text are truths regarding two of the most common errors husbands make in seeking to fulfill their role as head of the wife.

First, the phrase "lord it over them" conveys the concept of using personal power to force a weaker person to submit. Whenever the husband does that, he's using manipulation based upon his person—how loud he speaks, how he leans forward in a power stance, what he uses for a threat. Clearly, intimidation has no place in our portfolio of leadership tactics. There's a well-known secret about husbands who bully: When you fall back on this method of being the head, you're not leading from either love or strength, but from fear and weakness.

Second, the phrase "exercise authority over" refers to pulling rank, not genuine leadership. If things don't go according to his plan, this man will shout, "Listen, woman! Who's the head of this marriage anyway, you or me?" But this kind of leadership fails for the simple reason that no one wants to follow. Authority doesn't make you a leader; it only gives you the responsibility to be one. My advice to you is always to reach for the opportunity and never hide behind the label.

THE KEY TO HER HEART
(AND YOUR HAPPINESS)

So we know that the husband's role as head is to lead the wife in a way that promotes and enables her to achieve their joint goals. But what are his actual responsibilities?

A responsibility begins with an obligation for which you are accountable. No doubt that's why the New Testament teachings about a husband's primary responsibility are delivered as commands or imperatives:

- "Husbands, love your wives, just as Christ also loved the church and gave Himself for her" (Ephesians 5:25).
- "Husbands ought to love their own wives as their own bodies" (Ephesians 5:28).
- "Let each one of you in particular so love his own wife as himself" (Ephesians 5:33).
- "Husbands, love your wives and do not be bitter toward them" (Colossians 3:19).

> *Husbands are to love their wives. The breakthroughs start here.*
>
>

Immediately after noticing the tone of command, you'll notice the obligation, repeated over and over again: *Husbands, love.*

Why do you think the Creator of marriage would raise this responsibility to the top of the flagpole for the husband? Because it's the one essential, the master key that opens all the rest of God's best for men in marriage. Husbands are to love their wives. The breakthroughs start here.

Think about it: What single essential was your wife looking for in her husband? Read any women's magazine. Ask any psychologist. "That he really loves me…a lot."

God's plan for marriages that are made in heaven and enjoyed on earth requires the husband to realize that the most important responsibility in his whole marriage is for him to love his wife. Can you think of any other need that the wife would have that wouldn't be met if he truly loved his wife?

I think men have to be told to love in our marriages because this kind of love doesn't come all that naturally to us. Biologically, we're more geared for pursuit, for winning, for work, for pioneering, for sex, for protecting the young'uns back at camp. But genuine love—at least love as our wife understands and needs it? Now that's something we have to slow down and learn.

For example:

- Try to think like your subject to feel her feelings and dream her dreams.
- Ask, listen, and observe very carefully.
- Comb the Instruction Book.
- Practice.

Once we see our responsibility in this light, most men can really get into it. The husbands I admire frankly admit that they *study* their wife—put her under a lens, so to speak, and invest themselves wholeheartedly in learning her natural preferences, her innermost desires, and her deepest needs. For them, "Husbands, love..." has almost disappeared as a duty. Instead, it has become both the challenge and the privilege of a lifetime.

LOVE OF ANOTHER KIND

Learning to love a wife often leads a husband to the question, "But how do I love her if I don't feel anything?"

One good friend of mine had always struggled to love his wife. He felt that since the emotions of love were not present in his life, he'd be acting with hypocrisy to "fake love." For years his marriage labored under this seemingly logical yet fully unbiblical thinking. Only when he realized that genuine love is a choice, not an emotion, was he free to truly love his wife.

The problem for English speakers is that the word *love* is so frustratingly inexact. We use it for a host of applications: friends, grade-school crushes, chocolate sponge cake, sex, the Atlanta Braves. No wonder we're confused when we use it in marriage.

Fortunately, the Greek of the New Testament is more helpful. Two different Greek words can be translated into English as *love*—*phileo* and *agape*. (A third, *eros*, from which we get the word *erotic*, applies obviously to sexual attraction. Since you were thirteen or so, you've known that this biological impulse can exist quite apart from a relationship or even an actual person.)

Although *phileo* and *agape* love overlap from time to time, understanding their differences will help you see more clearly your responsibilities to love your wife:

1. *Phileo* requires two people to appreciate each other, and *agape* doesn't. *Phileo* is mutual in that both people must have some degree of respect for each other; *agape* may be entirely one-sided.
2. *Phileo* is conditional, and if certain conditions are not met, then *phileo* can end. *Agape* comes with no strings attached because it is based upon the internal commitment of one person to another, regardless.
3. *Phileo* relationships may last for a certain length of time, then stop due to changing circumstances. *Agape* exists, period. It is not related to time.
4. *Phileo* requires some level of emotional attachment and personal affection to thrive. *Agape* flourishes in the soil of commitment; any positive emotional experiences only enhance it.

5. *Phileo* can be a blend of both selfish and self-giving attitudes and actions. *Agape*, on the other hand, always seeks to benefit the other, often at the expense of self.

Now note this: When the Lord commands the husband to love his wife, the word He uses is the word *agape*, not *phileo*. Why? The Lord knows that any husband can choose to love his wife with *agape* at any place and at all times, regardless of what did or did not happen.

What we've learned from most of our earthly bosses, coaches, and trainers doesn't help here.

Our responsibility—"Husbands, love"— doesn't start with feelings (although in my experience, it always ends up there eventually). Rather, it starts with a decision to love; it is to be constant, unconditional, sacrificial, and without end. The promise of *agape* love is what swept your wife away in the first place. And it is the only kind of love which adds up to a great marriage. By God's design, expressing it fully and consistently gives you great power in marriage. Jesus loves His chosen ones like this, and He is every husband's perfect role model.

For years I tried to make my marriage add up with *phileo* arithmetic. I was under the impression that it was acceptable for me to withhold my love from Darlene if she acted in an unloving way toward me. I figured my love was exactly that—my love and not hers. When she acted in a way that I liked, then I would give her some love. When she really pleased me, I would give her a big hunk of it. In other words, my love was selfish and conditional.

Here again, men, what we've learned from most of our earthly bosses, coaches, and trainers, and what comes to us from our survival instincts doesn't help here. Those responses can keep you bitter, your wife unresponsive, and your marriage all shriveled up.

One day God showed me another set of numbers. I had come to understand and revel in God's sacrificial love for me. Just knowing that He was committed to me *especially* when I let Him down made me want to love Him and please Him all the more. Then I made an unforgettable marriage breakthrough—I realized that He wanted me to give to my wife the same kind of love. The choice was up to me. In fact, how I acted was entirely up to me and had nothing to do with her. She may or may not behave toward me in a way that I wished that she would, but I could always choose to act in a loving way toward her.

When I broke through to this understanding, my prospects for a great marriage shot up. I apologized sincerely for being stingy and manipulative with my love, and I told Darlene I wanted to change. Through tears, she gave me her forgiveness. Old wounds surfaced for healing. I committed to her on that day that I would accept with joy my responsibility— "Husband, love!"

Somehow, something was released deep inside when I came to understand that I could love Darlene with or without those unpredictable emotions of love—that the times I loved her when I felt least loving toward her may be the moments in which I loved her the most. As I relearned the habits of unconditional love, another relationship emerged right before my eyes. It was the marriage—and the wife—I had been trying to engineer all along.

Agape love is your calling in marriage, too. Your opportunity—the master key to breakthrough in your relationship.

And guess what? You *can* do it!

TURNING THE CORNER

At a conference recently where I taught these principles to two thousand men and women, I tried an experiment. I asked every man present to stand up beside his wife and sit only when I read a characteristic of true love that he couldn't seem succeed at with his wife. (I took the questions directly from Paul's well-known description of *agape* love in 1 Corinthians 13.) Here's what I read:

1. Do you suffer patiently when your wife is being difficult?
2. Are you kind, regardless of how unkind she is?
3. Do you refuse to envy her or anything in her life?
4. Do you make a point of giving her the credit?
5. Do you refuse to treat her rudely, in public or in private?
6. Do you choose to never demand that you get your own way?
7. Do you never express threatening or uncontrolled anger at her?
8. Do you never doubt her and wonder if she is really telling you the truth?
9. Do you never secretly celebrate when something bad happens to her?
10. Do you tell her the truth, even when it's difficult?
11. Do you bear whatever comes into your life?
12. Do you believe in her, especially when she doesn't?
13. Do you hope the best for her?
14. Do you endure and endure in your love for her?
15. Do you allow your love to never end?

You would have thought germ warfare had hit the auditorium. By the end of the second question, more than 30 percent were down. By the end of the seventh question, hardly any men remained standing. You should have heard the catcalls from the other men and the laughter from the women.

Then I asked the rather embarrassed men to stand up one more time. "This time, I want you to sit down only if you know beyond a doubt that you cannot really fulfill those characteristics of love," I said. "For instance, if you've had a problem getting angry at your wife, could you *decide* not to get angry with her if you so chose? If so, as I read each characteristic of love, please remain on your feet."

We went down the same list: patience, kindness, protection, trust.... Not a single man sat down. They all admitted, many for the first time, that it had always been in their full power to obey God's command to love their wives.

The same is true for you and me.

Where are you today, my friend? Do you need to turn a corner in how you are living out your role as head or your responsibility to love?

Remember, as you travel toward God in search of breakthroughs in your marriage, He's coming toward you also, longing to give you the desire of your heart.

Will you do your best to receive it?

Note: Walk Thru the Bible has a six part video series just for husbands who desire to maximize their marriage. Call 800-763-5433 for information about "Leading and Loving" or visit our Web site at www.walkthru.org.

Chapter Eight

The Heart That
Makes the Home

BREAKING THROUGH TO HELPING AND SUBMISSION

One warm evening on a visit to Hawaii, I watched a TV documentary on some of the most remarkable flowers on earth. Beautiful and rare, they cling to life on lava formations high in the mountains of Maui. But according to the narrator, these flowers were slipping into extinction, not because of their rugged habitat, but because a bird had disappeared from the islands—extinct due to human encroachment and the invasion of foreign species to this tropical paradise.

What, I wondered, *does a bird have to do with this flower?*

As the story unfolded, I learned that the rare tropical bird in question had an unusually specific job. It used to fly around the cliffs of Maui pollinating the equally rare flower with its uniquely shaped beak. That was its purpose. Beak to flower was an exact fit; the nourishment of nectar for the transfer of pollen, a perfect exchange. No other bird or insect could get the job done.

Now with the bird gone, the exotic flower was unable to reproduce, and it was about to go, too.

Enter men who would be birds. On the screen, two mountain climbers rappelled down a dangerous cliff. They each carried a long pole that ended in an odd-looking prong. "They are attempting to replicate the pollinating habits of the extinct bird," explained the narrator solemnly.

As it turned out, the dangling-men-on-ropes-with-poles approach wasn't much of a success, and the program ended with a glum prognosis for the mountain flower.

How amazing! Both that flower and the bird were created by God to live in a most unusual location and to flourish there by fitting together perfectly. Break the plan, and two beautiful creatures die.

A woman's rare and beautiful destiny in marriage has come under heavy attack.

Marriage is like that. When the Lord decided to create woman, he fashioned the wife with absolute perfection and with a specific purpose in mind. Everything that the Lord created in that woman—her abilities, impulses, and potential—was tailored to accomplish something special in marriage. Fulfill that role, and both the woman and the man will thrive. Discard it, and something beautiful disappears.

Unfortunately, like that flower-and-bird relationship, a woman's rare and beautiful destiny in marriage has come under heavy attack during the last fifty years, pushing biblical marriage toward extinction as a cultural norm. Even for contemporary Christians, God's clear guidelines for marriage can sound strange, unworkable, and even offensive.

Consider the wife depicted in media today: she likes to do lunch and shop. She's rarely at home with her children—if she even has children. She's emotionally unreliable, never at church (unless she's old, uneducated, or both), a schemer and a gossip, interested in her "personal journey" more than her marriage vows, and prone to emotional flings when unhappy with her husband.

But of course she has designer nails.

No wonder many wives Darlene and I talk to tell us they feel rudderless in a turbulent sea. They feel misunderstood, undervalued, overworked, and guilty. More than anything, they suffer from a sense that something beautiful and precious has been lost. And for every suffering wife, I'll guarantee you there's a suffering husband nearby.

What is a woman's role in marriage? What are her responsibilities toward her husband? And what happens when the God-ordained exchange breaks down?

These are the questions I want to explore with you in this chapter. In the face of these sobering issues, I first want to affirm for you that God has good news for your marriage. Let me hang way off that cliff, so to speak, and say something full of honest hope: It is the will of God that your marriage be full of joy.

Why am I so sure about that? Because God's plan for wives and husbands goes way beyond what merely works to what is beautiful, rare, and full of wonder and delight.

The only requirement for a life-changing breakthrough in your relationship with your husband is that you follow God's creation plan. Are you willing to do that? What will you do if you discover (or rediscover) in the next few pages a clear biblical teaching that radically disagrees with your current marriage habits?

My prayer is that you will have the courage to reach for God's best. You know by now that there's nothing like compromise to keep you in Chair Two—with all of the fall-out and losses that position entails. If you really think that your substitute plan will work, think again. Remember that lovely flower, fading from the islands. Listen to your neighbors, the news, your own heart. And pray, asking God to show you His breakthrough way.

I promise you He will.

The Wife's Role: Helper

From Genesis, we know that important aspects of man and woman are shared—both share the same value, and both share the same commission:

So God created man in His own image; in the image of God He created him; male and female He created them. Then God blessed them, and God said to them, "Be fruitful and multiply; fill the earth and subdue it; have dominion over the fish of the sea, over the birds of the air, and over every living thing that moves on the earth." (Genesis 1:27–28)

And yet, you don't have to read far in Genesis for an immediate and clear message about the woman's distinct role:

And the Lord God said, "It is not good that man should be alone; I will make him a helper comparable to him."…Then the rib which the LORD God had taken from man He made into a woman, and He brought her to the man. (Genesis 2:18, 22)

We saw in the last chapter that, though equal with his wife in value, the main role (purpose, goal) of the husband is to lead. The biblical term that describes the wife's role is the word *helper*.

This major distinction is revealed and supported throughout the rest of the Bible: the man's role from day one of the marriage covenant was to be the head; the woman's role from day one was to be his helper. Clarity about this is the foundation of a First Chair marriage.

The New Testament clarifies it further: "For man is not from woman, but woman from man. Nor was man created for the woman, but the woman for the man" (1 Corinthians 11:8–9). That means that before God even started creating the woman, He had an end in mind—and worked backward from there. When God decided to create woman, every genius of divine creativity went toward making one very particular kind of purpose and function—a helper.

God didn't say He was going to make Adam a housekeeper, a trophy, a sexual plaything, or a mother for his children. Rather, God revealed He had in mind a perfect complement who would be:

Sovereignly designed…
Equally loved…
Perfectly suited for the man's needs…
Mercifully provided for the man's loneliness…
Uniquely gifted to make a beautiful life together with him.

THE REAL MEANING OF HELPER

Do you ever feel that the person who receives the help is luckier than the person who gives it? Or that being a helper is not very exciting, maybe even demeaning?

Then take a look at who is described most often as helper in the Bible: God! Glance at these Scriptures and you'll see what I mean:

> So we may boldly say: "The Lord is my helper; I will not fear. What can man do to me?" (Hebrews 13:6)
>
> Nevertheless I tell you the truth. It is to your advantage that I go away; for if I do not go away, the Helper will not come to you; but if I depart, I will send Him to you. (John 16:7)

I can't tell you the number of husbands who tell me that their wives have no idea what they're going through.

The Lord is the great helper of the Bible. And Jesus' name for the Holy Spirit is Helper. Helping is an immensely powerful, meaningful, and divine task.

A helper is someone who comes alongside to meet the needs of another. She supplies what is lacking, nurtures, protects, and lends support where the other is weak or faltering. She is like the bird that enabled the flower to create a future.

As I traced the word helper through the Bible, I couldn't miss the fullness of its meaning—when the husband has a need, the helper's role is to bring all of the resources possible to fulfill that need quickly and fully. What a beautiful picture!

As you, then, consider your role as helper, you are fulfilling an important role that God Himself fulfills. Perhaps that's why Jesus taught that the greatest among us is the person who serves the most.

If the husband's welfare is the wife's main charge, then the most important question she should be asking him is, "How can I help you better than I am doing right now?"

I can't tell you the number of husbands who tell me that their wives *have no idea* what they're going through, what their deepest needs are, or where more support might be called for. Sometimes, of course, the husband needs to learn to talk more openly with his wife. But often the problem starts with a wife who is too focused elsewhere, trying to find achievement and fulfillment apart from her marriage and home.

Do you wonder how your husband feels about his marriage? About whether he feels supported, helped, and strengthened by you? There's only one way to find out—ask him. He might stumble and stammer around for a while, but listen carefully. Wait. With God's help and your prayers, he'll give you "helper pointers" that will radically change your relationship for the better.

Over the years, husbands have shared with Darlene and me some helps—or areas where help is wanted—that matter most to them:

- "I need to come home to a place of peace and order. The house doesn't have to be a showpiece—just a place where I can recover from a bad day without getting hit by more stress the instant I walk through the door. That's home to me."
- "I love it when Sandy touches me, rubs my back, stands close to me, that kind of stuff. Guys like that—at least I do. I carry a lot of tension in my shoulders and neck. Her touch is my medicine."

- "Please be more patient with me in social situations. Don't talk for me or try to 'fix me' in front of others."
- "When we go through tough times with bills or broken-down cars, my wife never makes me feel like a loser. Of course, that kind of support from her means the world to me."
- "We have kids, but I'm not one. Treat me like an adult—maybe even like a friend you want to get to know better. That kind of respect would go a long way."
- "A simple dinner with my wife and kids around the table. That's when family happens for me. We're all there and we're talking about whatever. We could be having beans and hot dogs, that part doesn't matter."
- "Ann-Lise does such a great job of caring about my sexual needs. She never shames me and never says no. I mean, a rain check is fine, but she knows how to make me feel wanted. I've talked to a lot of friends who are pretty miserable on this point."
- "My wife never tries to make me perform spiritually—like, how I pray, or when I speak up at church, or what I know about the Bible. I'm pretty awkward with this stuff, and she understands. That's cool. It actually helps me want to grow in my faith."
- "She cares about my hopes and dreams. She asks me about them all the time. I know they're right at the top of her prayer list, and she helps me watch for what God might be doing to help them come true."

I'll never forget the flood of appreciation and love I felt for Darlene the first time she told me she was going to fast for me all day. "You're not going to eat all day *for me*?" I asked, not quite believing what I was hearing. But she was serious. She knew I was facing some difficult matters in my work, and fasting was her way of saying, "I'm completely with you, honey. I'm going to be praying that the Lord will really bless you at work today."

When a wife truly sets her mind on helping her husband so that the Lord would nod His head in approval, then she moves into the realm for which she has been sovereignly created by our omnipotent God. In this realm, she is powerful, irreplaceable, and blessed. "She does [her husband] good and not evil all the days of her life" (Proverbs 31:12). She is in a perfect position to make all kinds of breakthroughs in her relationship with her husband. And she makes the miracle of marriage happen—as only a wife can—no matter where she and her happy husband make their home.

Even if it's on the side of a cliff.

> *She cares about my hopes and dreams. She asks me about them all the time.*
>
>

THE REAL MEANING OF HOMEMAKER

In Paul's job description for wives, we see that the main way a woman is helper to her husband is as overseer of a particular domain:

> That they admonish the young women to love their husbands, to love their children, to be discreet, chaste, homemakers, good, obedient to their own husbands, that the Word of God may not be blasphemed. (Titus 2:4–5)

There are few words that sound more quaint these days than "homemaker." It's right up there with "gentleman caller" and "doily"! But like the word helper, we need only to return to God's timeless Word to discover the true meaning of this role. The word here for *homemaker* is a compound Greek word from two common words. The first is the usual word for "home" or "house and its environs." The second is the word for "work" or "labor."

Now look at what Paul wrote to young Pastor Timothy: "that the younger widows marry, bear children, manage the house, give no opportunity to the adversary to speak reproachfully" (1 Timothy 5:14). In this case, the words *manage the house* give a fuller picture of what the Lord had in mind. *Manage the house* is a translation of another Greek compound. The first part is the normal word for house, but the second part will surprise you. It is the word for "despot." And a despot is someone with complete control.

I must admit, that word shocked me. The Lord not only instructs wives to be home-workers, but He also wants them to fulfill that calling with incredible freedom and power. That word was a breakthrough for me. Up to that point in our marriage, I thought that as the head of the home, I was the one responsible for the home but shared the decisions with my wife. But this verse taught me that I was wrong. Although the husband is the head of the wife, the wife is the despot of the home.

Although she is still under the covering of my final authority in the marriage, Darlene is commissioned by God to exercise her authority in the home. Generally, God sends the husband into the marketplace to provide for his family, but the wife is sent into the home to take charge of it completely.

Now I understand that a wife has her own leadership role—the house and its environs are her turf. If you doubt me, look for a moment at the Bible's most complete portrait of a wife at work in her role. You'll find it in Proverbs 31:

- "She brings her food from afar."
- "She also rises while it is yet night, and provides food for her household."
- "She considers a field and buys it; from her profits she plants a vineyard."
- "She perceives that her merchandise is good."
- "She extends her hand to the poor, yes, she reaches out her hands to the needy."
- "She makes tapestry for herself; her clothing is fine linen and purple."
- "She makes linen garments and sells them, and supplies sashes for the merchants."

- "She opens her mouth with wisdom, and on her tongue is the law of kindness."

God's description shows a person who is a marvel of abilities and influence at work—a businesswoman with employees, her own real estate holdings, her own ventures, and her own irreplaceable contributions to the quality of life of her family.

How incorrect it would be to say, then, that the Bible teaches against the working wife. In fact, the Bible teaches the opposite, but with clear conditions:

- her husband must be her first priority and receive the best of her energies and attention;
- her children must be her next priority, and she must be the primary worker in her home;
- her every other venture (and there may be many) should launch from her position of power and record of accomplishment at home.

Given the scope of a wife's mission in marriage, I sometimes wonder why any wife would want to leave her family and contribute all her skills and energy just to make another company or person rich. Of course, women are as gifted as men to succeed in the array of learning and working experiences that our world offers. And you may be a person whom God has called to express your talents outside the home in significant ways. Perhaps the realities of your family's income needs make some kind of work outside the home a necessity.

But the Bible's encouragement to you is this: Make sure you, your husband, and your family are not losing out on all the possibilities that God has in mind for you. By His sovereign, powerful, and loving work in your life, He's given you the mission of a lifetime. I'd paraphrase it like this:

"Go, fulfill My dream for your life by helping your husband with all the competence, capacity, creativity, and compassion that I have given you. As you do, every dream that I have placed deep inside your heart will come to fruition."

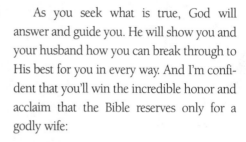

God's description shows a person who is a marvel of abilities and influence at work.

As you seek what is true, God will answer and guide you. He will show you and your husband how you can break through to His best for you in every way. And I'm confident that you'll win the incredible honor and acclaim that the Bible reserves only for a godly wife:

Her children rise up and call her blessed;
Her husband also, and he praises her:
(Proverbs 31:28–29)

THE WIFE'S RESPONSIBILITY: SUBMIT

For the husband, as we saw in chapter 7, the responsibility that grew naturally from his role as head was to love his wife. So if helping is a wife's role in marriage, what is her responsibility?

By the way, can you anticipate what the man typically desires most from his wife? In other words, what was the gift that you brought as "helper-in-the-making" that captured your husband's heart?

Your answer might go something like this: "Well, I was sure I'd met the catch of a lifetime. I admired and respected him, hung on his every word, I guess. We just loved to be together. In fact, when he proposed I told him I'd follow him to the ends of the earth—and I meant it!"

The result for him? He felt like he was king of the world. Your tender affection and fierce loyalty gave him an inner strength like he'd never known. That made taking the initiative easy.

Let's put it this way:

- God wired every woman to desire a husband who would be her leader while loving her more than anything or anyone else.
- And God wired every man to desire a wife who would honor, respect, and follow him more than anything or anyone else.

The biblical word for this gift of following and supporting in love is *submission*. Submission may sound weak, old-fashioned, or even vaguely offensive to you. But for your husband, a wife who chooses submission is his gold-plated invitation to success. After all, without someone who is willing to follow, how will his God-given role—"to lead"—work?

And what about for you? The Bible teaches that this principle of submission as your major attitude and responsibility toward your husband holds the secret of your success, fulfillment, and incredible influence in a godly marriage.

Your tender affection and fierce loyalty gave him an inner strength like he'd never known.

Precisely because the Lord created your husband to be the leader in your marriage, he longs for and is empowered by the affirmation, willingness, and unadorned loyalty he finds in you. Trust me, the loving will to follow he sees in *you* is the high-octane fuel that powers *him* to get out and lead.

Ask any man. With that kind of love, the ends of the earth are just around the corner!

On the other hand, I can assure you that nothing will frustrate, demoralize, and anger a husband more quickly or deeply than rebellion and disrespect in his wife. Nothing. When that attack comes from his kids, he feels challenged. But when it comes from his wife, he feels deeply betrayed.

Now let's look at what the Bible says:

Wives, submit to your own husbands, as is fitting in the Lord. (Colossians 3:18)

Wives, submit to your own husbands, as to the Lord. For the husband is head of the wife, as also Christ is head of the church; and He is the Savior of the body. Therefore, just as the church is subject to Christ, so let the wives be to their own husbands in everything. (Ephesians 5:22–24)

Nevertheless let each one of you in particular so love his own wife as himself, and let the wife see that she respects her husband. (Ephesians 5:33)

Likewise you wives, be submissive to your own husbands, that even if some do not obey the word, they, without a word, may be won by the conduct of their wives. (1 Peter 3:1)

If you thought that submission as a wife's major responsibility is merely one option for marriage, these verses should have changed your mind. Submission is clearly God's best for wives. If you are serious about a spiritual breakthrough to a Chair One marriage, submission to your husband is your privilege and your opportunity. Since creation day, it has been God's only plan for a wife who wants to please Him and realize His blessings in her marriage.

THE REAL MEANING OF SUBMISSION

I'm not sure about the grocery store where you shop, but at ours, you can't even get to the checkout stands without pushing your cart down magazine row. From nearly ever magazine cover, headlines tease and titillate tired housewives with a Madison Avenue gospel that couldn't be further from what we're talking about here. You've seen them—blurbs like:

"You can have it all—with or without HIM!"

"How to wrap him 'round your finger (and keep him there!)"

"Love 'em and leave 'em: what smart girls know about sex without regrets"

"Train your man to treat you right!"

If you take these flashy promises too seriously, you can go home with a migraine along with your noodles and asparagus. What if those women's magazines offered something different?

"Let him lead (you'll follow him straight to the marriage of your dreams)"

"'I was made to help him'": a happy wife's true story"

"It's sublime to submit—10 secrets smart wives want you to know"

My blurbs sound a little odd, don't they? And the magazines probably wouldn't sell, but at least they wouldn't be hawking illusions.

You see, what those magazine publishers don't know is that we never have to choose between a good life and God's life. Our God didn't cruelly set out to create a woman's role in marriage to tip the scales to your husband's advantage, to defraud you of a meaningful life, or to keep you from reaching your potential. God's truths are for our best, whether we're female or male, husband or wife.

Most of us have to first sort through many misconceptions that pass for truth before we can wholeheartedly move into a First Chair marriage. Over our years of counseling with couples, Darlene and I have noticed a number of common misconceptions about what it means to submit.

Misconception #1: A Husband's Job Is to Make His Wife Submit

Wrong! The Bible never teaches that the husband is to *make* his wife submit. Rather, the Bible teaches that the wife voluntarily *chooses* to obey the Lord and bring herself, as a submitted wife, to her husband.

The English word *submit* is another compound in the Greek, *hupotasso*. It combines roots meaning "under" and "to arrange together." In its narrowest definition, submit means to arrange all parts underneath. The wife, then, is to arrange all parts of her life under the headship of her husband.

This is why the Bible doesn't use a word like *obey* instead of submit. To submit to someone goes far beyond mere obedience. For example, you can obey another without bringing anything under his or her authority except that single act. Submission focuses on the deeper and more important issues of one's heart and intentions.

Think how dramatically this approach would change many marriages. Instead of a wife wrestling with whether or not she is going to submit in a specific matter, she would have already chosen to submit herself—even when she strongly disagrees with him (more on this hot potato). When the wife has broken through to true biblical submission as her commitment for a great marriage, then submitting in the range of different circumstances becomes so much easier.

> *Get those words in the hands of a man who confuses husbanding with absolute monarchy and you have a royal mess.*
>
>

Misconception #2: If a Wife Is to Submit to Her Husband "As to the Lord," Then She Must Act Like and Treat Her Husband As if He Is the Lord Himself

This misconception originates from that powerful nugget of a phrase in Ephesians 5:22—"as to the Lord." Get those words in the hands of a man who confuses husbanding with absolute monarchy and you have a royal mess. These husbands actually believe that they can hand down a decree and expect the wife to view every word as coming straight from the throne room of heaven.

Not a chance. As a Christian wife, you already love and serve one king, and the man in your kitchen ain't him! The phrase "as to the Lord" is meant to remind you that your choice to submit to your husband is a loving expression of your preexisting submission to Jesus, your one absolute monarch. The requirement of submission originated with Him, not your husband.

For those times when putting yourself under the authority of your 100 percent-human husband gets difficult, as it will, Paul encourages you to look right past him to Jesus and then submit anyway, "as to the Lord." Your response becomes a powerful expression of trust in God—that He stands behind all His plans, and that all His plans for you and your marriage are only for good.

Misconception #3: If a Wife Submits to a Husband "In Everything," Then She Must also Follow Him into Sin or Danger

Submission is an all-encompassing attitude and commitment that describes how you will relate to your husband. But does this commitment preempt submission to God?

Of course not. If Desperate Dan tells Edna Mae she must rob the corner market, she cannot obey his instructions. God said, "Do not steal." If Sleazy Sam tells Rosie to become a prostitute or to commit some other clearly immoral act, she is not free to obey his instructions. God said, "Do not commit adultery" and gave other commandments concerning sexual behavior.

The opportunity for the wife in these situations is to decline to do the wrong act because of her higher allegiance to God—without showing disrespect for the husband who is proposing it.

I don't suggest these guidelines lightly. God's principles for good marriages work even in times of severe testing. If you or someone you love ever faces this obstacle to submission, trust God to show you a way through. Know that the wife will probably face an unhappy husband. If he knows he's in the wrong, he's all the more likely to get defensive, accusatory, and angry. But as the wife remains respectful and calm, God's power is released to bring conviction, healing, and unity to the marriage.

And what about situations that threaten the wife with violence or danger?

Darlene and I have talked with many distraught women who face painful situations of abuse and degradation. The same principle holds true. A wife who is submitting to God can't cooperate with what God describes as sin. Paul's picture for Timothy of the man who is worthy of being overseer is that he be "not violent...but gentle, not quarrelsome..." (1 Timothy 3:3).

Darlene often reminds beleaguered wives that submission is not just what you do; it's an attitude of *wanting* with all your heart and will to honor your husband. Her encouragement to wives in these situations is always, "God is so faithful! He will show you how to be wise, care for your children, and still submit to your husband in a way that will be honoring to the Lord."

Misconception #4: A Wife Is Supposed to Submit to Her Husband, but He's Also Supposed to Submit to Her

Many young couples hang on to the idea of "mutual submission," a concept proposed from many well-meaning Bible teachers. This approach suggests that it's biblical for both spouses to be equally submissive to each other; or that sometimes the husband should submit to the wife, and at other times the wife should submit to the husband.

On the surface, mutual submission seems logical and fair. After all, no one can be right all the time. Proponents of this approach point to Ephesians 5: "And do not be drunk with wine...but be filled with the Spirit...giving thanks always for all things...submitting to one another in the fear of God" (vv. 18-21). But this passage is the conclusion of nearly five chapters of counsel to the body of Christ at Ephesus, wherein Paul is laying out what it means to be a Christian and how we should relate to each other *in the church.*

Submitting to one another, then, is addressed to individual believers in the context of the local church, not to spouses in the context of a marriage. In fact, in the very next verse, Ephesians 5:22, Paul switches from general instructions to specific ones:

1) for wives, submit (Ephesians 5:22)
2) for husbands, love (Ephesians 5:25)
3) for children, obey and honor (Ephesians 6:1)
4) for fathers, do not exasperate (Ephesians 6:4
5) for slaves, serve wholeheartedly (Ephesians 6:5)
6) for masters, do not threaten (Ephesians 6:9)

Then, commencing at 6:10, Paul again returns to general instructions in his familiar plea to all believers to "put on the full armor of God."

Context makes all the difference. In church, Jesus is the head—and believers without specially designated roles of leadership are to submit "one to another." But in marriage, God is clear: "Wives, submit to your husbands."

Just because you are the helper of the husband doesn't mean your husband shouldn't help you.

This doesn't mean that a husband cannot and should not help the wife or choose to follow her opinion. Just because you are the helper of the husband doesn't mean your husband shouldn't help you. When he does help, he's not assuming the role that the Bible has delegated to you; he's *assisting* you in your role.

Similarly, when he chooses to defer to your decision in a matter, he hasn't stopped being the leader but is hopefully exercising wiser leadership of the marriage by trusting in your judgment when you're the one in the position to make the best decision. After all, a mark of great leaders is knowing who can bring the best judgment to bear on the problem at hand.

Misconception #5. If I Submit to My Husband, Then I Won't Be Able to Voice My Opinions or Feel Confident That My Feelings and Ideas Matter

Submission is anything but passivity. What a destructive misconception that is! The whole point of your role and responsibility as a godly wife is to promote your husband's success and manage your home empire wisely. I believe if you're fulfilling your God-given role, your husband will not only realize but treasure the balance, wisdom, intuition, and different perspective you bring to the marriage.

But what if your husband is heading for trouble or treating you poorly but seems unwilling to ask for help? Again, the Bible supports your equal value, equal potential, and equal destiny before God. Your uniqueness is vital to the success of your marriage. Your feelings and ideas matter. That means you can disagree with your husband's conclusions and behavior. I guarantee it will happen. But what matters is *how* it happens.

Our suggestion is to ask respectfully, "Are you open to my ideas on this subject at this time? I think I can help." Or let him know, "Honey, I really need to talk through with you how I feel about this." You can be urgent and impassioned without trespassing on his role as head. Remember that a person who feels no threat will rarely react defensively. And no one is more gifted at opening up the most stubborn and unreasonable husband than a godly, submitted wife. If you sense that he's feeling insecure or manipulated, assure him that you will support him whatever his decision.

FLOURISH AND GROW

I can remember when Darlene experienced a significant breakthrough of submission in her life. More than fifteen years ago, through some wise counsel, reading, and prayer, she arrived at an important realization. Here is how she expressed it: "I am not responsible for Bruce's decisions. I am only responsible for my response to his decisions."

Believe me, not a week passed before she had her first opportunity to test her submission. On some point, I wanted to go left; she was sure we should go right. But when she saw that I had decided, she immediately moved over to my side of the decision. Not only that, but she threw herself into making my second-rate idea work.

Our relationship has never been the same. At the time, it seemed like someone had untied a line from the pier, and now our sailboat could catch the winds and sail forth.

I must admit that neither of us has always lived up to New Testament standards for our marriage. But as we've both tried, I can tell you this— we can hardly recognize our marriage from where it used to be. Darlene's devoted grasp on submission as her responsibility and gift to me has helped a beautiful marriage to flourish. Through her, I have been changed along with our kids, and through our marriage I believe thousands of others have been touched for God's glory.

That is every Christian wife's calling and purpose. Like the exotic flower and rare bird in Hawaii, a wife and husband were created to flourish—together.

Note: Walk Thru the Bible has a six part video series just for wives who desire to maximize their marriage. Call 800-763-5433 for information about "The Heart That Makes a Home" or visit our Web site at www.walkthru.org.

Chapter Nine

Turning from Treachery

BREAKING THROUGH TO LOYALTY

istress.

It has to be one of the all-time ugliest words. Yet one day more than twenty years ago, I came home from work and I heard that word spoken by my wife. And she was talking about me....

I could tell Darlene was distraught when I walked in. I had hardly put down my briefcase and loosened my tie when she started to pour out her feelings.

With tears welling in her eyes, she said, "You love Walk Thru the Bible more than me."

You could have knocked me over with a feather. My wife is not given to self-pity or sudden emotional breakdowns. After a moment, I sat down across from her.

"You really feel that way?" I asked.

"Yes."

"But I love you so much more than Walk Thru!"

"No, you don't," she said, unflinching. "You love your work more than me. She's your mistress. And since Walk Thru is what you do for God, I can't compete, can I?"

A knife seemed to plunge into my heart, and it was the knife of my wife's pain. "Sweetheart, please," I protested. "This isn't true. You know I love you!"

We talked for a long time. I tried to hear her out. I tried even harder to marshal evidence in my defense. But I couldn't change her mind or mend her heart.

That night I didn't sleep much. Far into the dark hours, with my dear wife turning fitfully beside me, I asked the Lord if what she had said was true. But I knew the answer even before I finished the prayer.

Your wife is telling the truth.

"What should I do?" I asked aloud in that quiet bedroom.

It's up to you.

I tossed and turned on my bed. I paced through the sleeping house. And by morning when I sat down to cereal and coffee across from Darlene, I knew I had to act. Little did she realize then that the marriage we shared was about to change radically and permanently...for the better.

> *Something at the core of the marriage commitment is broken or missing. A mistress of some kind has slipped in.*

You're reading this book because you want more. You want God's best. Specifically, you long for a thriving, fulfilling, and God-pleasing marriage. But if you're conscientiously seeking to obey the Lord by living out a biblical marriage and breakthroughs still aren't happening in your life, you may be suffering from a blindness similar to mine.

During these twenty years, I've discovered that thousands of apparently solid and even exemplary Christian marriages are in the same kind of trouble. Something at the core of the marriage commitment is broken or missing. A mistress of some kind has slipped in.

How easy it will be for you to skip over this chapter if you resist the possibility of emotional or physical infidelity of any kind in your relationship. Or if your personal commitments, like mine, seem generally laudable and even noble. But what I want to talk about is a blindness that keeps legions of husbands and wives stuck in the Second Chair year after year, wondering why things don't change for the better and spiritual breakthroughs don't happen.

Way back in the time of Malachi (about 450 B.C.), the temple was filled with diligent spiritual seekers, wondering how to break through. Something had gone wrong for them, too, but they just couldn't figure out what.

A VIOLENCE IN THE HEART

Their story is hidden away in the last book of the Old Testament. I think it's one of the most remarkable revelations in the entire Bible. Israel is enduring troubled times—God seems to be far away, crops are failing, the kids aren't turning out right. And like good children of Abraham, the Jews bring their woes to the temple. There they try to fix their troubles with tearful prayers, full offering plates, and more than a few sacrifices.

In the middle of this religious scene, Malachi shows up. He has God's answer, but it has nothing to do with the crops or the kids. In Malachi 2, the prophet sets the scene: "You cover the altar of the LORD with tears. With weeping and crying; so He does not regard the offering anymore, nor receive it with good will from your hands. Yet you say, 'For what reason?'" (vv. 13–14).

Sound familiar? It does to me. When we feel that something is wrong in our lives, many of us go to church more, give more, pray more. Then when nothing happens, we can get frustrated with God, even a little angry.

Malachi reveals the mysterious block in Israel's prayer life. What he says must have taken them by surprise: "Because the LORD has been witness between you and the wife of your youth, with whom you have dealt treacherously; yet she is your companion and your wife by covenant" (v. 14).

The reason the Lord refused to see their tears and offerings was because of what He saw in their marriages. The cover-up was over. God

Himself had taken up the role of witness, interrupting their impressive church service to make a public report:

You have broken faith with your wife.

Many versions translate the phrase "you have broken faith" as "you have dealt treacherously." Treachery—another ugly word—means to violate an allegiance or betray a trust. A treacherous stretch of river is characterized by hidden dangers, hazards, or perils. Treachery is the opposite of trustworthiness or loyalty.

Malachi has still more to say from God: "For the LORD God of Israel says that He hates divorce, for it covers one's garment with violence," says the LORD of hosts. (v. 16).

Now God's view of Israel's real problem comes into sharp relief. Husbands have dealt treacherously with their wives by breaking their vows. This act of betrayal, God says, is really an act of violence; that is, an act of force that injures or abuses another. The wayward husbands have sown disloyalty and reaped a catastrophe—for their spouses, their children, themselves, their families, and ultimately their nation.

One Sunday evening, the reality of this kind of violence struck home for me. I had preached on this passage at a large church in the Southeast. At the end of the service, hundreds of adults flooded to the front. Many were sobbing. I assumed that these were penitent husbands and wives who had divorced and wanted to find healing, but I was entirely mistaken. Without exception, every person pressing forward for prayer and comfort was an adult child of parents who had divorced. The pain in that group was overwhelming. Their injuries, some sustained in family breakups years and even decades before, went deep.

Finally a middle-aged woman spoke up: "You're the first person I've heard who described the violence of divorce on the children. I'm here because I've always felt guilty about my pain, like it was my fault, or like I shouldn't have felt so devastated. My parents said, 'Don't take it personally.' But they committed the violence directly against me!"

When I asked the crowd if "violence" was an accurate description of what they, too, had experienced, every head nodded in grim agreement.

I assure you, when the consequences of treachery in marriage are standing right in front of you, tears streaming down, you get a fresh perspective on why God hates divorce. He hates the pain and waste and injury it causes. But please don't think God hates the people who get divorces or the children of divorced parents. Not for a second! Those dear people—and perhaps you are one—God loves with an everlasting, passionate, and unconditional love. He is at work for them every day, bringing healing out of hurt and wholeness out of brokenness.

Let me ask you this: What does God want at the heart of your marriage instead of treachery? May I suggest two words? These two words are so powerful in releasing spiritual breakthroughs in Christian husbands and wives that they matter to you right now if neither the thought nor the reality of divorce has ever entered your marriage.

The words are *absolute loyalty*.

ROOM FOR JUST TWO

These are bleak days for loyalty. To most ears, the word sounds antiquated and stuffy. Loyalty is fine if you're a Boy Scout, but grown-ups suspect that it's probably a cover-up for weakness, soft-headedness, or insufficient ambition. How can you look out for number one, we ask, if you've traded away all your rights to someone else? Isn't putting yourself first, the therapists ask, the best way to ensure that you'll have something to offer your "significant other"?

Besides being unpopular, absolute loyalty in marriage is just plain hard to live by. No matter what direction you look, real and ever-present temptations woo you and your attentions. People, priorities, and pleasurable pursuits clamor for your time, your talents, your passions, your body. Promising careers beckon. Options for personal and intellectual growth seem to have your name written all over them.

But have you ever noticed something startling? *Most of what calls out to you offers room just for you, not your spouse.* The simple, though at times painful, requirement of every husband and wife is to insist on a no-division policy at every decision point. The two of you have become one, and anything that would try to pry you apart into two again is unacceptable. No person, goal, activity, or endeavor that would create a wedge is allowed!

Here's a rule of marital loyalty that I highly recommend: *Total marital loyalty does not permit any competition to make inroads into the relationship.* This means that your spouse will never again have to face competition for your complete devotion. This radical commitment—think of it as your covenant "adhesive"—will make your marriage soar to new heights.

Take a minute to ask yourself, "What is the biggest competition that my spouse has to wrestle with in order to have all of my loyalty?" Does your spouse feel second fiddle to your:

- work?
- recreation?
- television viewing?
- children?
- friends?
- investments?
- ministry?

> *The two of you have become one, and anything that would try to pry you apart into two again is unacceptable.*

Of course, a crucial area of loyalty in marriage involves sexual integrity. And I'm not talking only about the act of committing adultery. Sexual loyalty goes far beyond that. Many today try to separate the final act of sexual unfaithfulness from the times we practice *private unfaithfulness* in our imaginations, conversations, reading and viewing, or even physical touches. We don't want to accept that we've already driven a wedge of disloyalty and infidelity into our marriage when we see a person who really attracts us and we begin to daydream what it might be like to be in an intimate relationship with them.

Just imagine what would happen in those early stages of private betrayal if our spouse could read our minds, enter into our imaginations, or be introduced to our lusts. Imagine how betrayed he or she would feel!

In this area, I believe laws of natural consequences apply: private treachery always breeds public treachery; treacherous thoughts always produce treacherous plans; and treacherous plans always produce treacherous actions—and a marital slide toward divorce.

THE SEVEN STAGES OF MARITAL SLIDE

Over the years, I've found myself searching for a visual picture of how this slide from total delight to total treachery occurs in the average couple's marriage. Finally, while developing the *Biblical Portrait of Marriage* video course at Walk Thru the Bible, I came up with a model that has helped thousands of couples. Think of each stage as a box. As you read them, try to identify where you and your spouse are right now.

Stage 1: DELIGHT—The Never, Never Box

The first stage of delight surrounds the budding romance, engagement, wedding, and the early period of the marriage. You walk with your head in the clouds because that's where your heart is. Your marriage seems to be carried along effortlessly by a greater power. How wonderful to be in love!

You're convinced that your marriage must have been made in heaven. You can't imagine why anyone would have troubles in their marriage. And divorce? Break this remarkable union of harmony, love, and affection? Never!

This could be called the Never, Never box because at this point in your life and marriage, you'd *never* leave your spouse. Your vows are still freshly etched in your heart, and if there is something you are going to do right, it is going to be your marriage! You are utterly committed to never, never break your marital relationship or covenant.

THE SEVEN STAGES OF MARITAL SLIDE		
Stage 1:	DELIGHT	"Never, Never."
Stage 2:	DISCOURAGED	"Marriage is harder than I expected."
Stage 3:	DISILLUSIONED	"My marriage is boring and frustrating. It had better improve."
Stage 4:	DOUBLE-MINDED	"Dilemma of uncertainty."
Stage 5:	DESPERATE	"I'll try anything; I've got nothing to lose."
Stage 6:	DESPAIR	"Who cares what happens; I've given up all hope."
Stage 7:	DIVORCE	"Sever, sever."

Stage 2: DISCOURAGED—The Marriage Is Harder Than I Expected Box

Somewhere in the first years, your spouse stops bringing you flowers each week or serving your favorite meal in the candlelight. Neglect raises its ugly head and wounds your heart. You can't believe your spouse would ever desire something instead of you at every single moment of your marriage.

As time passes, you continue to discover ways either your spouse or your relationship doesn't live up to your expectations. Whereas you used to be blind to little irritants, now you can't stand the fact that he still leaves his socks on the floor or that she talks on the phone to her mother for hours on end. You become a candidate for disloyalty, but you probably don't choose it.

As disappointments multiply, you find it more difficult to overcome your emotional letdown. This fading fortitude and weakening courage is called "dis-*courage*-ment." Your marital stamina to keep working through problems weakens. This marriage thing certainly can be a lot tougher than you expected!

Stage 3: DISILLUSIONED—The My Marriage Is Boring and Frustrating and It Had Better Improve Box

You sometimes find yourself rising up with determination to "fix" your marriage and bring it back to those early, happier days of stars, laughter, and romance. At times you succeed, but now you have to work at it.

More often, your emotions bottom out. You skirt with depression. You say hurtful words in anger or from hurt, and unlike earlier days, sometimes you don't even pull them back or apologize. Your interests start to diverge, but instead of deferring to each other, you think your spouse is the one who should do the deferring. Without consciously choosing, you begin to put your personal interests and needs in first place—the early stages of treachery.

At times, you just want to escape. To do that safely, you spend whole evenings glued to the television with barely a word passed between you.

You're beginning to realize that things may never change. Hard realities rise up like granite walls. One day you find yourself simply accepting them—"This is my marriage; I have to deal with it." No more illusions, no more fairy tales. Now you're standing in the bleak sunlight of "dis-illusion-ment."

Stage 4: DOUBLE-MINDED—*The Dilemma of Uncertainty Box*

You begin to entertain thoughts that never surfaced earlier—do you really want to live the rest of your life like this, with this person? These thoughts are especially nagging in times of pain and loneliness. *Maybe, you wonder, I married the wrong person. Maybe I would be much happier with someone else, someone who would treasure me, love me, treat me special, find me irresistible.*

Uncertainty and doubt spring up like thistles. Suspicions and mistrust color your outlook and your choices toward your spouse. Even your ventures into kindness and affection are discredited by your doubts and hesitations. You seek sincerity but harbor insincerity. You seek integrity, but you cannot escape your duplicity. You are mired in the muck of "double-mind-edness." The spirit of betrayal (cloaked in rationalizations of self-preservation and practical thinking) sets up shop in your heart.

In the back of your mind, you start a pro and con list—reasons to stay, reasons to leave. Not that you've decided to leave, but you haven't decided not to, either. You wait for something final and irrefutable to make the decision for you.

Stage 5: DESPERATE—*The I'll Try Anything; I've Got Nothing to Lose Box*

Circumstances and emotions start to push you into a corner. At times you feel frantic. An invisible barrier separates you from your mate. Your face becomes drawn and you age almost before your eyes. At your feet lie previous failed attempts at reconciliation. In the middle of the night, your mind searches for a miracle, some path out of this pain.

Desperation leads you to behave in ways you never could have imagined. You plead with your spouse to go back to the church, walk the aisle, and renew your vows. You go back to the neglected, right path—seeking God's will, obeying His commands, following biblical guidance. Or you stray further into compromise, experimentation, and me-first choices. An emotional or physical relationship outside of your marriage may now feel irresistible; they may be just the tonic your marriage needs.

> *Maybe,*
> *you wonder,*
> *I married the wrong*
> *person. Maybe I would*
> *be much happier with*
> *someone else.*

Stage 6: DESPAIR—The Who Cares What Happens; I've Given Up All Hope Box

Even the desperate measures fail to bring life back to the dying relationship. You slide into dejection and finally the gloom of depression. Even your personality fades beneath the weight of the growing despair. Hope, what hope?

No longer do you resist the inevitable. No longer can you find the desire to work for change. This level of resignation actually brings some relief—at least you know the final outcome.

Now you're drifting. Any loyalty you might hold on to in the marriage would be for purely practical reasons—paying the bills, caring for the kids, getting through another day. You may drift like this, attached to your partner, for years—countless marriages do. But the marriage relationship itself is dead.

Stage 7: DIVORCE—The Sever, Sever Box

The end can come with a whisper or a bang, but one day you just walk away—literally or emotionally. Suddenly, what's in your mind now is not your life in the marriage, but your life after the marriage. Any verbal and emotional attacks now are both purposeful and powerful—you want to take your last stand, do your final damage. You need to stake out your position, assign blame, and convince yourself and others that what happens now is inevitable.

I believe a successful marriage is the result of falling in love over and over again— always with the same person!

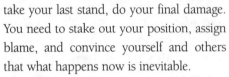

All that remains is to formalize the death and extend it from the personal into the public. It's time to choose divorce—or manipulate your spouse into choosing it for you. Either way, you're both outta here.

The violence seems complete, but in so many cases, it's merely spreading in wider and wider circles.

How tragic this slide from delight to divorce! And how incredibly painful, defeating, and deadening are the effects of disloyalty in the marriage covenant as it moves from treachery toward complete violence.

As you read through those seven stages from delight to divorce, you may have felt a little depressed. Perhaps you could identify with some or even all of them. Most happy marriages that I know have touched or lived through quite a number of those stages somewhere along the line. Some permit themselves and their relationship to continue sliding toward disaster while others choose to stop the process. Together, they begin to choose to change. They bravely climb back up that slide into the peaceful box of never, never.

Time and maturity and familiarity do change our marriage relationships, don't they? We can't stay in the wedding chapel forever. But the Bible gives us every reason to expect ongoing oneness, fulfillment and, yes, delight, in our marriages. I believe a successful marriage is the result of falling in love over and over again—always with the same person!

Now that kind of future in marriage is worth protecting from the dangerous slide. The Bible shows us where to start. And it isn't with flowers or chocolate or wealthy in-laws.

THE SECRET: YOUR SPIRIT AND HIS SPIRIT

Have you *ever* met an engaged couple who thought their marriage wasn't going to work? I haven't. We just don't enter marriage with unhappiness, much less divorce on our minds. Instead, we believe—no matter what Aunt Meg or the national statistics warn—that our marriage will turn out exactly the way we thought it would when we walked down that wedding aisle.

So what goes wrong? What can we do to keep the seeds of division, treachery, and betrayal from sprouting and taking root in our marriage? Let's look again at the passage in Malachi. God tells us He hates divorce because of how it happens (treachery and betrayal) and because of its consequences to people (violence). Then He reveals His solution for safeguarding a thriving, enduring marriage: "Therefore take heed to your spirit, that you do not deal treacherously" (Malachi 2:16).

In other words, from the Lord's perspective, the most strategic influence over anyone's marriage is the condition of his spirit. God points to the core of our being (our highest security command central) and says, "Guard yourself!"

The consequences of living on guard are enormous. Take my marriage, for example: Regardless of Darlene's actions or attitudes, I retain the full responsibility and power to guard my spirit and remain absolutely loyal to our marriage covenant, resisting all compromises and competitors.

Ultimately, we can't control much about our spouses, can we? But keeping a watch on our spirit is both entirely possible and entirely up to us. And the condition of our spirit will determine whether we choose to be treacherous or absolutely loyal. Solomon recognized this when he wrote: "Keep your heart with all diligence, for out of it spring the issues of life" (Proverbs 4:23).

Over the years, I've counseled innumerable couples, and I've come to the same conclusion: Marital unhappiness, strife, and unfaithfulness all come from the same source—an out-of-control inner being, an unguarded spirit.

What happens to men or women who don't rule their own spirit, who allow their spirit to freely roam wherever and whenever it pleases? Proverbs paints a most disturbing picture: "Whoever has no rule over his own spirit is like a city broken down, without walls" (Proverbs 25:28).

A city without walls is totally indefensible against anything that seeks to enter, overthrow, conquer, or control it. When a husband doesn't rule his spirit, it's like he has torn down all his home's walls, ripped out its burglar alarm system, swung open the doors, and declared to all passersby that his marriage is fair game for a hostile takeover.

Once I attended the annual meeting of a large Christian association. The two thousand pastors and parachurch leaders who gathered nearly filled the high-rise hotel. For three days, we met from morning till night. We prayed, sang, and talked together about changing our world for God's glory. The whole conference was nothing short of impressive.

But after I got home, a friend who had attended with me called to say he had a different perspective on the event. He told me he'd been witnessing to the executive manager of the hotel. During the conference he'd talked with the manager about what a remarkable difference Christ had made in his life and in his family. The man seemed to be warming to the gospel—that is, until checkout time.

My friend was waiting at the hotel front door for a ride to the airport when the manager walked up. He seemed distant, perhaps depressed. As the taxi arrived, the manager blurted out what was bothering him. "I just got the records from the convention," he said. "Your group of ministers filled nearly every room we had. But I'm confused. Can you explain to me why more than half of the rooms last night watched pornography?"

How tragic! By choosing not to control their spirits, these men had not only tarnished their Christian witness, they had dealt treacherously with the very wives they claimed to love.

How could such a thing happen? Believe it or not, many Christians don't seem to believe it's really possible to "rule" their own spirit. We've bought into a cultural lie that we're pawns of our passions, slaves to our present circumstances, victims of our pasts. But since the Bible commands us to "guard," "rule," and "take heed to" our spirit, we must conclude that the Lord has not only delegated that responsibility to us, but also given us the power to succeed at it.

"The fruit of the Spirit is...self-control," writes Paul in Galatians 5. Whereas the Old Testament shows that everyone must try to "guard their spirit," the New Testament reveals that the real source of self-control for the believer is the Holy Spirit working powerfully in tandem with our spirit and will.

> *By choosing not to control their spirits, these men had dealt treacherously with the very wives they claimed to love.*

The longer I live, the more amazed and thankful I am that the Lord granted to each of us the power and privilege to "rule our spirit," to "walk by means of the Spirit," and "be filled with the Spirit" so we will have the fruit of self-control. This personal freedom is a fragile and priceless gift from the Lord.

FIVE WAYS TO GUARD YOUR HEART

Let me suggest some practical, marriage-affirming ways to let this gift of self-control and godly freedom flourish in your marriage.

1. Restrict Your Life to the Never, Never Box

Although this may appear overly simplistic, there's one irrefutable, universal way to never slide down those harmful and self-destructive stages in your marriage, and that is to decide wholeheartedly you will not ever leave the never, never box!

This is what I call *volitional loyalty*. Volitional loyalty is based on the fact you have a will, and you can make a choice about loyalty. Too many of us believe the tragic lie that our marriage partner or some life circumstance can push us out of that box. But there's only one way to get out of the never, never box and it is to climb out by your own choice.

> *Be careful about sharing your personal disappointments or needs with someone of the opposite sex.*
>
>

Have you made up your mind about where you stand in relation to that box? Have you told your spouse?

I remember going to my mother-in-law and saying, "I want to tell you something. I'll never leave your daughter, no matter what happens. You can count on it."

Ever tell that to your wife? Your children? I recommend it. When you do, the Lord will rejoice and your spouse and children will be surely moved to higher, more secure territory—far from the threat of violence.

2. Relinquish Every Competing Person, Activity, or Goal

As we've already noted, early on in your marriage, only your spouse had your interest and your time. Sometime later, however, other people and opportunities vied for your attention. And let's be honest, don't some of these competing interests seem more compelling than your spouse at times?

Your answer has to do with your level of *emotional loyalty*. How can you know if you have crossed that invisible line when competition has won your heart and you've become disloyal? I advise spending time thinking, praying, and conducting a brutally honest inventory.

But your best help here is going to be your other half. And don't wait for a tearful confrontation to hear about it like I did. Just ask her or him. "Do I treat you as the most important person in the world to me? Are you my number one?" Sorry, but their answer *is* the answer.

Be careful about sharing your personal disappointments or needs with someone of the opposite sex—and never let any shortcomings in your marriage be the topic. Remember, God made us so that intimate conversation leads quickly to emotional bonding.

3. Restore Your Spirit by Staying in the First Chair

Here's one common rationalization that has been bought by the Christian marketplace: "My spiritual life doesn't have anything to do with my marriage. If we talk together, keep the peace, don't get into too much debt, attend church, and don't sin too much, our marriage will be just fine."

But this is wrong. Biblically speaking, the number-one solution to marital problems is for the individuals to grab their hearts, resolutely move them right back to the First Chair and tie them, nail them, glue them, and even staple them down. I call this practicing *spiritual loyalty* in marriage.

Humble your heart before God, repent over your personal sin, rebellion, and selfishness, and do exactly what the Lord says to do—and you'll learn firsthand the incredible miracle that the Lord unleashes in the marriages of those who live life His way.

Ask God to show you any areas where you especially need to guard your spirit or exercise more self-control. He will—and He will show you simple steps toward victory if you ask and obey.

4. Rekindle Your Sex Life with Intimacy, Never Pornography

Healthy intimacy is a powerful bond between the married partners, while adultery, including pornography, is a powerful destroyer. Consider the severe consequences attached to this warning against sexual infidelity: "For this is the will of God, your sanctification: that you should abstain from sexual immorality…that no one should take advantage of and defraud his brother in this matter, because the Lord is the avenger of all such, as we also forewarned you and testified" (1 Thessalonians 4:3–6).

God demands our *physical loyalty* to our spouse. Describe a policy for how you're going to set a course for success in this area, and share it with your spouse. With forethought and a few simple rules, you can both steer clear of a world of hurt. For example, how will you touch someone of the opposite sex? No touches at all? only a hug? Will you close the door if you're in your office alone with "competition" for your spouse? How about meals and business travel? Again, I urge you to set a course for *absolute loyalty*.

Healthy sex in marriage is meant to be a loving pleasure, shared affection, meaningful intimacy, and affirming experience. As Genesis 2:24–25 says, "Therefore a man shall leave his father and mother and be joined to his wife, and they shall become one flesh. And they were both naked, the man and his wife, and were not ashamed."

Finally, if the quality of your sexual experience together is a sore point, don't invite more trouble by doing nothing. Seek counsel from your pastor; an older, mature Christian friend of the same sex; or a Christian counselor.

5. Remain Committed to Your Covenant and Spouse

Covenants in the Bible are either conditional or unconditional. A conditional covenant is fashioned around the formula, "If you do this, then I will do that." In other words, if you fulfill your end of the bargain, then I'll guarantee a certain response; if you don't, then I don't have to deliver. (God's covenant with the Israelites before they entered Canaan was conditional; see Deuteronomy 29.)

An unconditional covenant, however, operates on unconditional loyalty—without any contingencies. You state it, "I will…period." (God's covenants with Noah and Abraham were unconditional; see Genesis 9 and 15.) In this covenant, one party commits to certain actions irrespective of the attitudes, response, or merit of the other party.

What kind of covenant did you make at your wedding? Did you commit "to love and cherish you if you continue to love and cherish me"? Or "to keep myself only for you as long as you don't gain forty pounds"? Or "to honor you as long as you make money and buy me nice things"? This may be news to you, but if you celebrated a Christian wedding, then you agreed to a totally unconditional relationship that would last till death.

The moment you face the radical nature of your marriage vows and radically assent to their terms, your marriage will surge with new life.

You have no idea how many Christian couples muddle along suffering and complaining because the little boat of their marriage barely floats, *but one or both partners are half in the boat and half in the water!*

The moment you face the radical nature of your marriage vows and radically assent to their terms, your marriage will surge with new life. Why? Because your choices and expectations are now being determined by your vows, not by your spouse. There'll be no room for vengeance and thus withholding your love (no one is keeping score). No room for meanness or selfishness in order to make the other person pay (no debt is owed). Instead, you'll be free to love your spouse at all times with tenderness and goodwill.

MORE THAN ANYTHING ELSE

The more you understand and grasp the incredible power of the unconditional covenant you and your life partner have made, the more reason you'll have to remain in that never, never box forever.

Tie yourself into that box, my friend. Take off your traveling shoes and nail yourself into that box. Pour superglue up to your ankles. Tie unbreakable ropes to every one of your thoughts, ambitions, and imaginings. When you do, some amazing things will happen almost immediately. You'll not only bring great joy and peace to you and your spouse but also to your children and grandchildren. You will bring honor and pleasure to your Father in heaven. And in nearly every case, you'll become a candidate to *receive* the same quality of love you're giving away—and that's probably what you were looking for in the first place.

Which brings us back to what I told Darlene after her revelation to me that I was seriously compromising my relationship with her. I thought long and hard. I prayed. I calculated how I spent my days, my hours, my energy, my money. I penciled out different scenarios. And not long afterward, I sat down with her and spelled out my loyalty to her.

"Darlene, what you said about my having a mistress must be true," I began. "I didn't realize it, but I see that you are right. Now I need to prove to you and to me that this no longer will be true. So starting today, I'm canceling all speaking engagements for at least a year. I will be home from work at five o'clock every single night."

Darlene looked at me to be sure I wasn't suffering from an old-fashioned Georgia sunstroke. But I wasn't finished. "And we are selling our house and moving to the country so we'll have some fun things to do together as a family. Honey, I'm not upset or angry or bitter," I continued. "You were right and I was wrong, and I'm very sorry. When the time comes that you feel that you are number one to me again and Walk Thru is number two, please tell me. But I will never ask you."

And that's what happened. We sold our house in a development and bought a farm in the country with a little two-bedroom house. I was home every night at five, and I disappeared from the speaking circuit for a year.

During that time, a breakthrough took place in our marriage. All outside compromises and competitions had been stripped away. No ministry "mistress" came between us. Yet I never felt locked up or victimized. With every passing day, I became more convinced that this kind of "forsaking all others" was what I needed to do. And in the fertile soil of this severe loyalty, my heart and hers became one.

One day we were walking in the woods along the shore of a pond. Darlene said, "Bruce, I think it's time for you to travel again. There are a lot of good reasons for you—for us—to be doing that."

"Do you really mean it?" I asked.

"Yes, I do," she said. Then she held my hand and said the words I'd been waiting to hear. "And I know you love me more than anything else in the world."

Note: Walk Thru the Bible has a four-part, hard-hitting video series in the Biblical Manhood Series entitled "Personal Holiness in Times of Temptation" which reveals God's answer to temptations of sexual immorality. Call 800-763-5433 for information.

Experiencing Breakthroughs in Your Parenting

Chapter Ten

God's Big Idea for Moms and Dads

BREAKING THROUGH TO THE NEXT GENERATION

The early '70s was a time of beginnings for us. Freshly married, Darlene and I were starting our family and our life of ministry together. We were on the front end of a lot of learning curves back then. Maybe you've been there—your dreams are as big as a Greyhound bus, but you're still riding a tricycle. One thing we knew for sure—we wanted to make our futures count for God.

During that time, I remember signing up for a secular management training conference. I scribbled notes furiously during the seminars and offered up fervent prayers during the breaks. In the middle of one session, a friend I was sitting next to nodded to the next table. "See that guy over there in the red tie?" he said. "He's Dr. Johnson's son."

I couldn't believe the coincidence. Frederick Johnson (not his real name) was a renowned Christian leader, practically a household name at the Wilkinsons'. Here was his son, and this wasn't even a Christian conference. What a terrific opportunity to pick up some insights on both family and ministry in one conversation.

At the first break in the program, I hurried over to introduce myself. We chatted briefly about the conference, then I said, "I understand you're the son of Dr. Johnson?"

"Yup, I sure am," he replied, smoothing his tie.

"Listen, I'm just getting started, so I'm curious," I continued. "What was it like growing up in the home of such a famous Christian leader?"

I'll never forget what I heard next. The man's demeanor changed abruptly and a volley of swear words shot out of his mouth. After he cursed his father and everything he stood for, he lit into his mother. Then he launched into a vigorous and hate-filled attack on Christianity. By then his face was nearly as red as his tie. All I could do was try to listen.

Every year, sincere, dedicated First Chair Christians are raising kids who will end up compromised Christians.

When he had finished, he gathered himself, spun on his heels, and left. Later, when I asked about him, I was told he had checked out of the conference.

I went home the next day with a binder full of ideas on management, but my heart was full of something else—deep sorrow and mortal fear. Over dinner with Darlene, we talked long and soberly about Dr. Johnson and his angry son. We couldn't imagine a worse outcome in our life together than a child rebelling so completely and bitterly against both us and God.

How can we pass along our legacy of faith to our children? That, in a nutshell, is the determining question for each of us as Christian parents. Not surprisingly, the editors of *Christian Parenting Today* magazine report that of the thousands of parents they poll annually, failing at that challenge continues to be their readers' single greatest fear.

The urgency of making a spiritual breakthrough in your parenting comes from a dismaying fact: every year, sincere, dedicated First Chair Christians are raising kids who will end up compromised Christians, even some who will turn against the Lord.

But it doesn't have to be so. My purpose in this chapter is to help you make sure that never happens in your family. When the Lord invented human beings, he created children to be completely helpless without a parent's constant intervention. In fact, he created human offspring to be the most helpless for the longest time. When you combine a child's needs with today's worldly influences, a parent's task can feel like a losing proposition.

Yet God didn't make a mistake. He had a specific purpose and plan in mind. If we can understand and put into practice our God-intended role and purpose as a mom or dad, we can parent with confidence. We don't need to live in fear of raising lost, angry, unbelieving children.

By now you have a sense of the progression of this book: one desire, one choice, one arena at a time, we are moving toward complete possession of our lives for God. In Joshua's day, the campaign was about taking cities. For us, it is about making key spiritual breakthroughs. The prize?—God's "promised land" of blessing for us and our children and our children's children.

My breakthrough challenge for you in this chapter may require courage:

When you understand clearly what God wants for you as a Christian parent, will you be willing to make whatever change is necessary? Will you take steps to bring your parenting beliefs and behaviors in line with God's revealed plan?

If your answer is yes, the prospects for the next generations in your family are very promising indeed.

GOD'S BIG PLAN FOR PARENTS

So what is God's big plan for parents?

Once again, the answer is in God's conversation with the Israelites through the prophet Malachi. As we saw in the previous chapter, the Jews were upset because God wasn't answering their prayers. They felt beleaguered, stymied, followed by a cloud of misfortune. God's surprising response to their complaint was that their troubles could be traced straight to broken marriage vows. Interestingly, in the course of the Lord's rebuke of their marriages, He reveals His special creation day assignment for man and wife as parents:

> Did He not make them one? Having a remnant of the Spirit? And why one? He seeks godly offspring. Therefore take heed to your spirit, let none deal treacherously with the wife of his youth." (Malachi 2:15)

Did you catch that? On creation day, God set in place a big idea, a master plan, and He put it in the safekeeping of two people—a father and a mother. He didn't just put this plan in place for the selfish pleasure of the couple in question either. He wanted something. He was waiting for it, counting on it, and depending on it so that the rest of his plan could work: Through the union of man and woman, He was seeking godly offspring.

Notice that God's top reason for the marriage union did not include:

- taking advantage of the "married, head of household" tax deduction;
- getting invited to more dinner parties;
- combining incomes;
- sex;
- making babies with the same last name; or
- raising well-adjusted, educated, and successful children.

Rather, in God's mind marriage was to be the starting point for populating the world specifically with humans who would love God and serve Him.

That's why I can tell you that what resonates so deeply in your heart is merely confirmation that you are awake to God's grand idea for you. The Lord wants you to have full integrity and to walk worthy of your calling—and then bring your boys and girls right along with you. They are to be walking in your footsteps, embracing your values, serving your God, choosing your Lord to be their Lord. Yes, it is our Lord's desire and plan and expectation that you will pass the torch of godliness to the next generation!

Remarkable, isn't it? I mean, God could have minted godly offspring like bright copper pennies, millions upon millions of them, with no significant job description for Mom and Dad at all. Instead the Lord created an incredible, self-propagating, parent-dependent method of producing an ever-expanding population of men and women who belong to Him.

God's internal means of gaining worshipers (godly families producing godly offspring) potentially far outdistances God's external means (missions and evangelism). But the glory of this plan is also its vulnerable point: the role of the father and mother.

Just think what would have happened if Adam and Eve and all their descendants would have obeyed the Lord. Godliness and harmony would have spread around young earth instead of debauchery and darkness. In Genesis 6, we read that "every inclination of the thoughts of [man's] heart was only evil all the time" (6:5). Something had already gone terribly, unfixably wrong. And God had to start over.

The Bible is really the record of a heartbroken Father starting over many times in His passionate effort to bring home His lost kids. ("The heart of the gospel is the pain of God," wrote one theologian.) And in His quest for global godliness, He asks of every new mom and dad the same question: "Will you fulfill My plan for you and pass on the legacy of godliness to the next generation now cooing in your arms?"

Think of that legacy of godliness as the inheritance you have amassed for your children or as your family's most priceless heirloom.

Think of it as a baton in a relay race. Have you ever watched a relay event at a track meet? In a relay, a team of sprinters works together to get a baton from starting line to finish line in winning time. As one runner approaches the end of his or her lap, the next runner in the rotation sprints up to full speed alongside. As they converge, the first runner reaches forward with the baton while the fresh runner reaches back to seize it. When the baton changes hands, so does the race. The race isn't over until all four sprinters have completed their laps—and nothing counts unless the last runner carries the baton across the finish line.

A relay event has always struck me as a powerful illustration of parenting. Success for us as mom and dad isn't just about how well we run as individuals, but about how well we pass the baton. And only when the story of the generations who follow us is told will our "win" at raising godly kids be known.

Success for us as mom and dad isn't just about how well we run as individuals, but about how well we pass the baton.

The psalmist captures this parenting relay race beautifully when he prays:

O God, you have taught me from my youth;
And to this day I declare Your wondrous works.
Now also when I am old and gray-headed,
O God, do not forsake me,
Until I declare your strength to this generation,
Your power to everyone who is to come."
(Psalm 71:17–18)

Look at the movement of the baton of faith in these verses: As a child, the psalmist received it, and "to this day" he's experienced it personally, but his purpose for receiving the baton won't be accomplished until he's passed it firmly into the hands of "everyone who is to come."

This is God's "big idea" for us as Christian parents, and I believe it is your heart's desire for your family. Yet even a quick look around reveals batons getting dropped. We see families everywhere sliding into compromise. We meet adult children of Christian parents who reject the faith or spout only resentment and rage about his or her legacy.

So we have to ask, Why doesn't God's plan for parents always work? Why, in fact, does the line of faith often seem to weaken with each succeeding generation?

Part of the answer lies in the principle of the generational slide, which I introduced in chapter 2. As you recall, when we lined up Abraham's and David's family lines, what emerged was a disheartening pattern of steady turning away from First Chair living.

| First Generation | Second Generation | Third Generation |
First Chair	Second Chair	Third Chair
Joshua	the elders	the next generation
Abraham	Isaac	Jacob
David	Solomon	Rehoboam

There's no denying that the tendency of generations over time is a slide away from God. Yet the Bible is also full of family-affirming stories of parents who changed history by passing on the legacy of godliness to their children. Read about Boaz and Ruth, who were the great-grandparents of David. Or Hannah and Elkanah, whose radical obedience to God helped shape the prophet Samuel. Or the simple devotion of Elizabeth and Zechariah, who brought up John the Baptist.

In your desire to be a First Chair parent, you are joining with God's exciting plan to shape the future for him—one toothpaste smile, one peanut butter kiss at a time.

Let's look more closely at what you can expect.

THE JESUS EFFECT (A MAGNET IN THE HOUSE)

If you grew up in a truly committed Christian home you understand the incredible influence and attraction Christ offers. As your parents not only loved you, loved each other, but also loved God, you would find yourself strongly attracted to that which they found attractive. The joy that you sensed in them would be the joy you'd want for yourself. The enduring wisdom they found in God's Word would naturally become the starting point for your life choices.

"What remains most strongly in my memory of growing up is my parents' genuine joy about serving God," says a friend of mine who grew up in a missionary family. "My dad used to say, 'Son, I've got the best job on earth!' He never got over how blessed he was to be serving God. That kind of example lasts a lot longer than words."

Do you know what happens in this type of committed, but not perfect, Christian family? The children decide to accept Jesus Christ as their personal Savior. The faith and vitality of their parents' faith in Christ and relationship to Christ works like a magnet ever drawing them toward that life-changing decision—and forever out of Chair Three (estrangement from or conflict with God). Evidence shows that between 80 and 85 percent of these children come to personal faith very young—before thirteen years of age.

And the long-term outcome, I firmly believe, is even more stunning than that. *The Salvation Outcome Observation:*

> If your children grow up in a truly committed Christian home where you as the parents have a close relationship with the Lord and genuinely seek to serve Him, your children will come to know Him as personal Savior 100 percent of the time. After polling hundreds of

thousands of people around the world, I have never personally found one exception to that fact.

Mind you, I am not aware of any Bible verse that makes that claim. The closest we could come might be Proverbs 22:6—"Train up a child in the way he should go, and when he is old he will not depart from it." But I feel safe in saying that although there may be an exception, it is going to be an extremely rare one. Here's what I ask:

Evidence shows that between 80 and 85 percent of these children come to personal faith very young—before thirteen years of age.

If you were raised in a born-again Christian home by parents who not only loved the Lord and had a meaningful relationship with Him, but also served Him with genuine commitment in the ebb and flow of normal life, and you or any of your brothers or sisters did not come to the place where they put their trust in the death and resurrection of Jesus Christ as the full payment for all their sins and sole hope for salvation, then please raise your hand or come and tell me after this session is over.

In Johannesburg, South Africa, not one person in 3,000 raised a hand or came to me after the meetings. In Detroit's SilverDome, not one in 80,000 did. Nor in Singapore's largest church. Nor among the Wheaton College student body. Nor when I asked the question at national conventions for the Christian Businessmen's Committee or the nation's Christian teachers. Not one.

Okay, you can tell I love to ask that question! I find so much encouragement in the evidence. And I hope you do, too.

Yet from here on, I'm sorry to say, the generational evidence starts to lose its luster. As we noted in chapters 2 and 3, too often the children of First Chair parents have only "seen the works of the Lord," not personally experienced them. This secondhand quality about their faith makes the children of First Chair parents tend to ride along on the parents' spiritual coattails. When the kids grow up and have to make choices for themselves, they tend to show their true colors. It's Second Chair all the way.

Not only is this next principle true biblically, but my experience in ministry validates it at every turn. *The Commitment Outcome Observation:*

Although 100 percent of the children of committed Christians apparently become born-again believers, a relatively small percent choose to become as committed to Christ as their parents—and an even smaller percent choose to become even more committed than their parents.

You can see why Second Chair parents almost always raise kids who are worse off spiritually then they are.

As much as we would wish it to be otherwise, our church pews are full of evidence to support that principle. A genuine salvation experience, even one in a First Chair home, just doesn't always produce men and women who are committed wholeheartedly to serving the Lord.

For this reason, I encourage dedicated Christian parents to make it their family goal to raise children who will pick up their legacy of faith intact *and take it further.* I really think God's idea is that our legacy should grow, not dwindle, in worth and influence as it is passed along. This didn't happen for the people in our diagram of the generational slide. But it can happen for you as it has for countless others.

A DISINHERITANCE OF SONS

Try to imagine for a moment the vast difference between growing up in a family where the father and mother have a personal, enduring, and dynamic relationship with the Lord and live joyfully committed to Him and His Kingdom, and growing up with a father and mother who know the Lord, but only superficially, and live their lives committed mostly to themselves and their desires. Think of what you would grow up to expect of God.

Spiritually, life in the second family would be like…

1) standing beside a fire that puts out no heat
2) listening to a symphony with plugged ears
3) trying to get through a date with a guy who says he's crazy about you but all he talks about is Molly, Molly, Molly

God's laws of the spirit don't exist in a world apart from how he made us to think and react as humans. You can see, then, why Second Chair parents—distracted by other priorities, mired in compromise, characterized by mixed messages—almost always raise kids who are worse off spiritually then they are. These are the "church kids" who abandon Christianity early in adulthood and may not pick it up again until later, if ever.

Of course, children of First Chair parents can rebel or just slide. And children of Second Chair parents can move solidly into the First Chair. But in both cases, the children have to defy their parents' dominant life message and the accumulated influence of their upbringing to get there. The fact is that an overwhelming majority of children who grow up in Christian homes but choose to forsake the Lord are children of Second Chair—not First Chair—parents.

In one of the most heart-wrenching stories in the Bible, we're told about a Second Chair parent who raised Third Chair children. Eli, Israel's high priest, raised two sons who served under him as priests. But they rebelled against their father and the Lord. Their story begins in 1 Samuel

2:12 with the words, "Now the sons of Eli were corrupt; they did not know the LORD." They blatantly used their position as spiritual leaders to extort bribes and sexual favors.

But when Eli learned about the scandal, he only rebuked them weakly. God was offended. Through a prophet, he told Eli, "Why do you kick at My sacrifice and honor your sons more than Me...?" (2:29). Then God describes His reaction to Eli's sin of compromise: "Those who honor Me I will honor, and those who despise Me shall be lightly esteemed" (v. 30).

The story only gets worse. Eli's sons died in battle, and when Eli heard the news, he fell backward off his chair and broke his neck. Then enemy troops captured the Ark of the Covenant. The pileup of calamities prompted Eli's daughter-in-law to go into early labor. As she was dying in childbirth, she told the midwives to name her son, Ichabod, which means "the glory has departed."

The story's a brutal one, I know, but you get the picture. The accumulation of a parent's compromises will frequently lead to a family's spiritual ruin. I hope you noticed that Eli didn't put the Lord first for a very contemporary-sounding reason—he put his kids and their happiness first. But only sadness resulted. Both sons had died spiritually long before they were killed in battle. In trying to pass on a legacy to his sons, Eli had utterly disinherited them.

Are there understandable, but potentially deadly reasons you might be missing the handoff in passing your heritage of faith on to your children?

TALKIN' IN THE KITCHEN

Most of the parents I know do their clearest, most honest thinking about their families over coffee in the kitchen. Trusted friends stop by. The children drift outside to play. Pretty soon the grown-ups are leaning forward over the yellow kitchen table pouring out their hopes and fears for their kids.

Let's do some "talkin' in the kitchen" ourselves. I imagine you may be wrestling with a question or two. God's Spirit is at work in your heart, and the gears of your own common sense are turning. After teaching this topic to thousands over the years, I know there are touchy spots and areas of possible confusion:

"You make it sound like I'm responsible for my child's spiritual life and choices. Isn't this a personal thing that each child must decide?"

Yes, every person on earth must ultimately make his or her own choice to respond to God. But if we weren't responsible in a special way for our children's spiritual future, the Lord wouldn't relate the "godliness" of our children to us so directly. If we as parents weren't able to make key commitments on behalf of our children, Joshua could never have said, "As for me *and my house,* we will serve the Lord" (Joshua 24:15, emphasis added). The Bible's advice to us would read more like, "Raise your kids as best you can so that when they're ready to decide, they can respond to God's desire for godliness in a way that suits them."

God not only holds us accountable, but our children may be the most objective test of the spiritual state of our walk with God, our marriage, and our family. When the Lord laid down the requirements for leadership in His church, He revealed specific characteristics and requirements: A bishop then must be one…who rules his own house well, having his children in submission with all reverence (for if a man does not know how to rule his own house, how will he take care of the church of God?) (1 Timothy 3:1–8).

> *Our children may be the most objective test of the spiritual state of our walk with God, our marriage, and our family.*
>
>

Besides being blameless and gentle, a church "father" must have proven himself in his own home before he should be invited to lead in the Lord's church. The test for "rules his own house well" is the behavior of his children. But you can only be tested and held accountable for a task if you had been given the responsibility for it ahead of time.

Okay. But isn't this a dangerous idea? Is it fair to judge a Christian by their kids?

Let's always be careful not to set ourselves up as judges of our brothers and sisters. The line of accountability runs from the parent to his or her Lord, period. When I'm talking about using the Three Chairs principle to help you take a reading on your spiritual commitments, my prayer is that you will allow God to use that in your life and in the lives of those you're directly responsible for.

We all know families who endure great pain because of straying children and broken relationships. How God's Father-heart breaks over these hurts, too! Most people I know have more pain and more problems in the area of family than any other. And there's more guilt surrounding this issue of raising children, and how things have actually occurred, than any other subject I speak about.

Always look with grace on others. It only takes about a few days of trying to raise a child to know God before every Christian parent is pleading to Him for mercy. Diagnosing the family next to us in church is a deadly trap and a waste of time.

But my kids are already grown, and I see areas of serious failure. Is it too late for me?

Friend, the Lord has led you tenderly and firmly to this very place. God is waiting to restore and redeem—His very name is Redeemer (how much Satan must hate that fact!).

My encouragement to you is to repent of each sin right now. That's how cycles of failure are broken. That's what invites God back into the process of legacy building. Tell the Lord, "I'm sorry, I didn't do what was right. I did what came easily. I lived for myself. For all these reasons, I did not work at producing godly offspring as you intended for me to do. I really messed up. Please forgive me and show me what to do next."

Get yourself and your marriage into Chair One—and start all over. It's never too late to begin to influence your children. You still tower like a giant over their lives—and a humble, learning, seeking, and God-honoring father or mother of whatever age is the most towering influence of all.

What if my spouse and I don't even have or want kids? Is our marriage pointless in God's eyes?

So many young people that I meet today don't want to have children. They ask, "Can you imagine bringing a child into this dark world today?" But God says that's the whole point. You're supposed to bring children of light into the world to push back the darkness. I urge you, instead of reacting out of fear or convenience, reach for the fuller purposes God has to use your marriage and your home to impact the world for Him.

What happens if you can't have children? I know this is often an excruciating circumstance for husbands and wives. But consider this—I know many couples who can't have children who adopt or foster-parent children. I know one infertile couple who have—count them—thirty kids that they're "parenting" indirectly through purpose-filled (and fulfilling) ongoing relationships. What God wants from you as a husband and wife is still the same—godly offspring. Right in the center of God's will for your marriage you'll find your greatest joy, I promise.

But how can my influence begin to compete with all the other influences out there in the world?

Almost every sociological study that I am familiar with has summarized their research on this topic in the same way: A parent has by far the greatest influence—greater than friends, school, or media—in determining the character and direction of the child.

The question isn't whether you have influence over your child, but what kind of influence you exert and for what ends. God's plan is that your influence would be so attractive and compelling that your child leaves your home with heaven's designation of "godly offspring."

Have you made a purposeful and lifelong choice to "raise godly off-spring"? Well over 90 percent of all Christian parents have never made this simple, powerful declaration. And without a deep heart commitment to embrace the Lord's goal for your children, every other move you make will weaken and wander off course. Mom or Dad, my encouragement to you is to take a finish-line mentality—invest every shred of your energy and dedication to seeing your children cross the finish line for God.

After you've accepted this divine role as a parent, you'll find yourself in an exciting place—lined right up with God's biggest dream for you and your family. And you'll be ready to talk about the practical how-tos of raising godly kids. Now that you know your role, what are your responsibilities? As you'll see in the next chapter, God makes no secret about them.

Chapter Eleven

Masterpieces in the Making

Breaking through to Godly Parenting

*N*ear where I used to live in Oregon, a ninety-year-old man turns kindling into music. "Doc" Renno jokingly calls himself a wood butcher, but the world knows him as a first-rate violin maker (a luthier, to be exact). Renno's workshop is a quiet place, but every stick and chisel and glue pot there is about making sound.

"You don't know till you finish one if you've got a violin or kindling," he likes to say. "But a great violin has a soul. How to explain that, I don't know. It comes from deep inside."

If you've ever heard a master violinist or fiddler draw a bow over strings, you know what Renno is talking about. From a lovingly shaped contraption of wood and strings comes music that makes your spirit soar.

Sometimes raising kids strikes me like that. A lot of raw material—gap-toothed smiles, sticky doorknobs, blaring radios, long bouts of carpooling, bikes in the driveway, piles of laundry—but we're up to something more than making kindling. We're patiently, passionately tending something deep inside each of our children...a masterpiece.

How much Darlene and I want our children and grandchildren to be beautiful instruments in the hands of the Master! We want each of our offspring to be "handmade"—shaped intentionally, patiently, and skillfully (as God's Word guides us) to be all that they can be for God.

Can you think of any measure of earthly success that would mean more to you than success with your children? Even for the high-powered executives I've interviewed in countless training sessions, the real bottom line of success is not numbers, but names: "my wife, Connie"; "my boys, Trent and Chad"; "what happens when I walk through the front door of my house at quarter to six—that's what matters most to me."

I can't tell you how many times in counseling sessions I have heard heart-broken parents say, "I'd give everything I have to get my son back, to have another chance." If your children were alienated and living on the edge of destruction, you'd give every cent, every investment, every shred of reputation to guarantee their personal, emotional, and spiritual liberation.

> *We have to be careful in our parenting that what we say we want matches what we're doing to make what we want happen.*

With the stakes so high, why do so few Christian parents make a First Chair commitment to raise children in complete obedience to God's teachings?

As you'll see, too often we rely on hope and good intentions rather than God's plan for parenting as revealed in the Bible. Just look around and you can see how "what comes naturally" is getting good families in trouble.

Unlike Doc Renno and his violins, we can *know* how our kids will turn out if we follow God's instructions for raising godly children. I believe that by the end of this chapter you will have a clear, radical, and life-changing breakthrough in your parenting because you will have discovered what it really means to raise godly kids.

ARE YOU DRIVING ON AUTO-PARENT?

Ever met someone who was always talking about how much he wanted to be rich someday, yet you noticed he never did anything to make it happen?

Instead of getting serious about earnings, savings, and investments, he just talked—or maybe bought a lottery ticket now and then.

We have to be careful in our parenting that what we say we want matches what we're doing to make what we want happen. Otherwise, we're fooling ourselves. The Christian community is packed with parents who talk and pray and worry and give testimonies about raising godly kids. But if you look past the words to the actions, you see that they don't really connect.

These good people are raising kids on auto-parent. They're creating a home life by default instead of on purpose. They're reacting automatically instead of intentionally. Listen, this confusion of words (or stated beliefs) with actions is a terrible deception—and it's always dangerous! When parents on auto-pilot don't get what they say they want with their children, they often question the validity or practicality of their goal, or—worst of all—the truth of God's love and power, while remaining blind to what they have done to put their family in the ditch.

In my experience, auto-parents tend to travel down several distinct roads. I've identified seven parenting styles where the parents' *real* belief systems (forget what they say in church for a minute) could be paraphrased like this:

Style 1. The close-your-eyes-and-hope-for-the-best parent. Raising kids is basically a biological enterprise, according to this level-headed mom or dad. Like raising beans. So take care of the basics and nature will take care of the rest. Clothe, feed, and shuttle them around—and in due season you'll have a good crop.

Style 2. The here-you-take-them-and-make-them-behave parent. Raising kids is primarily a management problem for these task-oriented parents. They've learned the secret of maximizing their efforts—delegate. In the case of children, that would mean baby-sitters and child care, getting them enrolled in the right school, signing them up for Scouts, sports, and church camp. If problems surface, the solution is sure to lurk "out there" somewhere—a counselor, treatment program, eventually the U.S. Army. Hopefully, the child won't notice the missing ingredients—mom and dad.

Style 3. The my-kids-deserve-nothing-but-the-best-and-lots-of-it parent. Money talks for this parent—child-rearing is mostly a financial problem—and purchases turn into their main language of love, too. The signs show up early—with designer nurseries, enviable fashions, and sure-to-be-talked-about toys. The best remedy for dissatisfaction or stress is usually more of something at the store.

Style 4. The I'm-sorry-I'm-too-busy-working parent. Smart children in this family will swipe their parents' daily planners because in this home, raising children is a scheduling problem. Without an appointment, the child is mostly "out of mind" to the parents. Why? For this parent, work and job advancement is the measure of success. Without career success, how will they ever pay for Junior's college? As long as no crisis or catastrophe is underfoot at home, everything must be fine. Now, back to the office....

Style 5. The keep-them-under-my-thumb-until-they're-on-their-own parent. Raising children is a policing problem. External behavior matters—all that talking and feeling stuff is just for the movies. These sergeant-at-arms parents run a tight ship thanks to a well-honed arsenal of rules, punishments, detention, criticism, threats, bullying, manipulation, and general snooping around.

Style 6. The lock-them-in-church-every-time-it-opens parent. For this parent, raising children is a protection problem (or maybe it's just a storage issue). The solution? Keep 'em in church. Prospects for success go up in direct proportion to how much time the children spend in church and church activities and how little time they spend anywhere else. Problems slip in when this parent uses church time as punishment. But, on the whole, the parent-church alliance seems sensible. In theory, bugs that cocoon on church walls always turn into beautiful butterflies.

Style 7. The run-them-everywhere-and-play-everything parent. The minivan-taxi-service parent experiences raising children mostly as a transportation problem. After all, lining up a full calendar of terrific activities and making sure the kids get there is what makes a successful family. Sports, music, drama, ballet, cooking, woodworking, tae kwon do, youth group—these exhausted parents figure that busy kids won't have the energy or time to get into trouble.

Do you recognize a little bit of yourself or others you know in these descriptions? I believe these truth-deficient parenting approaches are basically Second Chair parenting wisdom. In fact, underlying each one is a sinful compromise of some sort: slothfulness, self-centeredness, greed, worldliness, fear, religiosity, and irresponsibility.

Do you need to make a break away from a Chair Two parenting approach? Try a personal inventory: Setting aside for the moment what you say to yourself and others that you want, evaluate your parenting convictions based on performance and activities alone. What one sentence would you use to describe your *real* belief system? What one word would best describe you?

Now I want to help you bring together as rigorously as possible what you desire as a Christian parent and what you do to make it happen. Trust me, this is an enormous leap forward.

Let's put the question in simple terms: "How can I by word and deed actually raise godly, committed First Chair children who will please God, make my heart sing, and—when I'm old and wrinkled up like a prune— make my whole life feel worthwhile?"

SEVEN STEPS TO RAISING GODLY CHILDREN

It's interesting—the same moment we choose to fulfill God's desire in our family by producing godly offspring, God immediately redirects our focus from our children to us, their parents! That's because God never starts with consequences but with causes. And godly parents cause godly kids.

This rule is simple, but often inconvenient. Want to see an important lesson bounce right off the head of your son? Try to teach him something that, in your heart, you don't think *you* need to know. Your words will snap back into your face so fast you'll think they were attached to a bungee cord. But your child is not being stubborn and difficult, just smart. He's watched you like a hawk since the crib. And since you've decided (by your actions, not your words) that what you are trying to teach him isn't very important to you, he concludes it would be pointless to apply it to him.

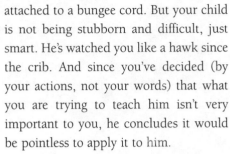

God never starts with consequences but with causes. And godly parents cause godly kids.

My friend, start here...in your own heart.

First Step. Love the Lord with All Your Heart

Personal godliness—for us and our kids—is always rooted in a living, breathing, flourishing relationship. And that kind of relationship never starts with behavior or requirements. It starts in the center of your being.

Let me tell you the secret of a great teacher. At Walk Thru the Bible we've trained over 50,000 professional teachers and 50,000 lay teachers, so I have some experience here. *Powerful teaching is not, ultimately, about the teacher's techniques; it's about the teacher's heart.* Nothing will influence a student more immediately and more profoundly than the heart of the teacher. The genuine passions, the driving commitments of the teacher— these are like the electricity that turns everything else on in the classroom so learning happens.

As they watch you as their parent devote your time, invest your money, and apply your talents to the work of the Lord, they too are attracted and compelled to do the same thing. If, on the other hand, you are devoted to chasing the American Dream, they'll be attracted to that, too.

Moses talks about this electricity in his famous parenting lecture, found in Deuteronomy 6. Here, after reviewing the Ten Commandments,

Moses tells the Israelites that the only way they'll possess the land and enjoy long life is to pass God's teachings on to "your children and their children after them" (v. 2). But notice how the parent's personal, passionate love for the Lord comes first: "You shall love the LORD your God with all your heart, with all your soul, with all your might" (Deuteronomy 6:5).

"First, make sure your heart longs for God and God-pleasing behavior," says Moses. "Make sure that the power is turned on!" Only then does he go on to urge parents to teach this same priority to their children.

Does it surprise you that the Lord doesn't instruct us in this passage to "Love your children with all of your heart, soul, and might"? I think it's because if our driving commitment is love of our children instead of love of our Lord, we will fall short of passing on our legacy. We will then, quite naturally, only seek to meet the needs of our child rather than obey the directives of our God—from which greater commitment comes our children's true best.

One of the hallmarks of men and women in the First Chair is that they love Jesus Christ. Trust me, it's not their good behavior, their busyness in church, or how much they know about theology. As these influencers mature, their love for Christ invades every motivation, priority, activity, and relationship. Loving him with all their heart, soul, and strength becomes a reality. And every person around them—spouse, child, friend, student—is sparked into a fuller life for God.

That's electricity! And your children won't wake up to godliness without it.

If God really has your heart, your heart will attract your children's heart like nothing else on earth. Then you'll be ready for the Lord's next step to successful parenting. In the second step, the spotlight is still on you, the parent.

Second Step. Know and Obey God's Word Yourself

Right after telling Israelite parents they must start by loving God, Moses tells them they must love His truths. Only as God's commandments are fully applied in their own lives will they succeed in passing godly living on to the next generation:

> And these words which I command you today shall be in your heart; you shall teach them diligently to your children, and talk of them when you sit in your house, when you walk by the way, when you lie down, and when you rise up. You shall bind them as a sign on your hand and they shall be as frontlets between your eyes. You shall write them on the doorposts of your house and on your gates. (Deuteronomy 6:6–9)

I love the way this passage gives such a vivid picture of how central God's Word is to be in the lives of parents. Are you supposed to tattoo a Bible verse on your biceps or paint the Ten Commandments on your mailbox? I don't think so. But God's truths—His very words from the Bible—are to be almost that apparent everywhere in a Christian family.

How important really is the Bible to you? If we based our answer on how many Bibles we owned, most of us would score pretty well here. Yet the real issue isn't how many Bibles we own, but how much of us the Bible owns. And ownership is nearly impossible to hide. For example:

- Do your children catch you reading the Bible on your own initiative?
- Have you started a conversation with them recently that connected a Bible verse to a question of the day?
- Do your kids know that God's Word is the joy of your heart, like it was to Jeremiah (Jeremiah 15:16)?
- When a behavioral or value question arises, do you lead the way to Scripture for your family to find God's standards?

A friend told me he prays every day that he'll fall in love with his wife—and he says his marriage is already blessed with affection and companionship. "Don't just wait for the feelings and the motivation," he advises. "Ask for them. And then ask for more!"

I like that approach. So I say to you:

- Do you desire to love God with all your heart, soul, and strength? Tell Him you don't love Him as much as you want to. Ask Him to grow that passion in your heart. Ask Him every day!
- Do you desire to hold up His Word and His teachings in the most visible and dynamic ways possible in your home? Tell Him you don't cherish His word enough for yourself, much less your kids. Ask Him to change your heart. Ask Him to show you how. Ask Him every day!

If you're having trouble getting the Bible habit started for yourself or your family, I encourage you to pick up a Daily Walk Bible, or subscribe to one of the Walk Thru devotional magazines. We've sent out more than 100 million magazines to encourage believers just like you. For a detailed plan, see my book, *Personal Holiness in Times of Temptation,* page 216 and following.

More than anything else don't wait to start. As you take those first sincere steps into God's Word, He will begin to infuse your life with strength and wis-

> *God has had your mission of raising godly kids in His mind from the beginning of time, and He wants you to succeed even more than you do.*

dom. The electricity will come on in your life. How do I know that? Because God has had your mission of raising godly kids in His mind from the beginning of time, and He wants you to succeed even more than you do.

Now you're ready to turn your attention from yourself to your kids.

Third Step. Tell Your Children Frequently of God's Works

This step surprises people. Maybe it's because we live in a time where giving public testimonies has fallen out of favor. Church leaders tend to think that declaring His Word through preaching and teaching is enough. We've forgotten that what we know of the works of the Lord directly affects the success or failure of our walk of faith.

By works, the Bible means exploits. Accomplishments. Answers to prayer. Intervention. Miracles. You see, God wants His record known and appreciated, not hidden, misinterpreted, or forgotten. If you've personally experienced God's works, you can stand up and tell anyone, "You gotta hear what God did in my life. It's changed everything!"

The Bible shows us what happens when the awareness of God's deeds fades. Let's return to our Joshua story for an example. As you remember, one of the key differences between the three generations was how they were related to the "works of the Lord."

The Joshua generation experienced and participated in the "works of the Lord" themselves; all those divine interventions during the wilderness years and the conquest of Canaan were part of their life story.

The elder generation grew up seeing and hearing about God's provisions and power. With the death of the first generation, however, those works became memories, not determining life events.

The third generation grew up with only second and thirdhand accounts of God's works. What kind of testimony could they pass along? Not much except doubt and uncertainty. Look at what the Bible says: "When all that generation [of elders] had been gathered to their fathers, another generation arose after them who did not know the LORD nor the work which He had done for Israel" (Judges 2:10).

Do you see why I'm convinced that the likelihood of choosing godliness is in direct proportion to how experientially aware a person is of past, present, and even future "works of the Lord"?

First Chair parents love Psalm 78 because it so clearly describes how God wants His exploits talked about in families. The whole psalm is a recounting of things:

> Which we have heard and known, and our fathers have told us.
> We will not hide them from their children,
> Telling to the generation to come the praises of the Lord,
> And His strength and His wonderful
> works that He has done....
> That they may set their hope in God,
> And not forget the works of God,
> But keep His commandments.
> (Psalm 78:3–4, 7)

The pressing reason to preserve this testimonial, the psalmist declares, is that things have gone terribly wrong in the past on this very point:

> And may not be like their fathers,
> A stubborn and rebellious generation,
> A generation that did not set its heart aright....
> And forgot His works
> And His wonders that He had shown them.
> (Psalm 78:8, 11)

As a mom or dad who takes this spiritual strategy seriously, you'll be following in the tradition of great leaders of the Bible. Do you want to be mentored in testifying to God's works? Start with Moses' fatherly exhortations in Deuteronomy (especially chapters 6–8, 11, and 28) and Peter's sermons in Acts (chapters 2–4). Make sure you let your children know that the God who walks with them in the halls at the junior high school is the same God who led Israel with pillars of fire and cloud through their wilderness years.

The next step is to span the chasm of time from past to present by never missing an opportunity to tell your children what God is doing in your life, your family, your finances, your heart and mind *right now.*

And like Israel, make a memory marker of God's works in your family. For you it might be a photo on the refrigerator, a verse on the dashboard of the car, a thanks offering at church. After the miraculous crossing of the Jordan River by the entire nation of Israel—on dry riverbed—Joshua instructed a person from each tribe to take a stone from the middle of the Jordan and build an altar. Listen to the reason:

> When your children ask their fathers in time to come, saying, "What are these stones?" then you shall let your children know, saying, "Israel crossed over this Jordan on dry land"; for the LORD your God dried up the waters of the Jordan before you until you had crossed over, as the LORD your God did to the Red Sea, which He dried up before us until we had crossed over, that all the peoples of the earth may know the hand of the LORD, that it is mighty, that you may fear the LORD your God forever. (Joshua 4:21–24)

Fourth Step. Teach Your Children God's True Word

When parents think of raising godly children, they immediately think of this particular step—teaching the Bible to their children. Once again Psalm 78 provides helpful insight:

> For He established a testimony in Jacob,
> And appointed a law in Israel,
> Which He commanded our fathers,
> That they should make them known to their children;
> That the generation to come might know them,
> The children who would be born,

That they may arise and declare them to their children.
That they may set their hope in God,
And not forget the works of God,
But keep His commandments.
(Psalm 78:5–7)

There's no doubt that it is the job of us as parents—not the priests, kings, or prophets—to teach God's truth to our children. Why? Because when our children learn from us, they will more readily move beyond just knowing to obeying.

Deuteronomy 6 presents four different levels or types of "teaching" our children the Word of God:

1. "You shall *teach them* (the law) diligently to your children" (Deuteronomy 6:7a).

This refers to formal teaching where you as the parent have an agenda and desire to teach something specific. For instance, this morning over breakfast, I read and discussed Colossians 1 to our eleven-year-old daughter, Jessica, before she left for school. The time was 6:30, the place was the breakfast table, the agenda was similar to what it was every school morning, and the teacher was seeking to fulfill the "teach diligently" responsibility.

2. "You shall *talk of them* when you sit in your house, when you walk by the way, when you lie down, and when you rise up" (Deuteronomy 6:7b).

This refers to the informal teaching which goes on naturally during the day. This type of teaching will be casual and unscheduled in response to our children's initiative. As you become more skilled at this, you learn how to transition the conversation back to the Bible through a natural question or statement. If the child doesn't pick it up, it's often not the time or the place to continue.

3. "You shall *bind them* as a sign on your hand, and they shall be as frontlets between your eyes" (Deuteronomy 6:8).

To the Jew, this type of teaching occurred when they wrapped small pieces of Scripture to their hand or forehead in one way or another to remind them of its meaning and importance. Today many individuals wear some kind of pin or jewelry that carries a Christian message—tastefully presented yet unmistakable to the observant individual.

4. "You shall *write them* on the doorposts of your house and on your gates" (Deuteronomy 6:9).

This refers to "teaching" which is more public and visible. If I walked through your home or workplace, how many different "write them's" would I discover on your walls, in your CDs, in your bookcase, on your refrigerator, or in your office? The Bible encourages us never to hide our light under a bushel, but to let it shine from the top of the mountains.

It's clear that God wanted the parents to teach all the time, in one way or another.

No mention of synagogue, church, Bible camp, or baby-sitter. All those avenues for teaching the Bible are certainly valuable, but only the teaching role of the parent is indispensable. The power to reproduce godly offspring remains primarily with the parent who loves the Lord, knows and obeys His Word, and is committed to the depth of his heart to produce godly offspring.

It's clear that God wanted the parents to teach all the time, in one way or another, and to demonstrate that their faith not only was private but also public. As you think of expanding the influence of your own parental teaching, could you add to your verbal or nonverbal communication either through private, personal, or public avenues?

Fifth Step. Lead Them to Accept Jesus As Their Savior

Ask any Christian parent—one of the greatest moments is to lead your own son or daughter in their prayer for salvation. "Actually, we were sitting on the stairs talking. I know I didn't say all the right things, but Kelly was so ready," one mom told me. "She wanted 'Jesus inside'—that's how she put it. I'll never forget that sweet moment."

A First Chair parent is being prepared every day by the Holy Spirit to be the host or mediator or go-between for a child who is waiting to meet God personally. And as I mentioned earlier, this nearly always happens before adolescence.

Some parents are concerned about the validity of their children's salvation experience, especially if this occurred very early. But remember Jesus specifically said, "Let the little children come to Me, and do not forbid them…" (Matthew 19:14). On another occasion, Jesus was even more pointed about the capacity of our young children to exercise saving faith: "Unless you are converted and become as little children, you will by no means enter the kingdom of heaven" (Matthew 18:3).

You can lead your child into God's family simply and lovingly. Build your conversation around basic truths, and the choices they invite for your child:

- "Jesus loves you and wants you to belong to Him forever."
- "But bad thoughts and wrong things that you do keep you away from Him. God's word for this problem is sin."
- "God loves you so much He already sent His son Jesus to save you.

Jesus lived a perfect life and died on the cross to pay for and take away your sin."

- "But you have to choose this gift for yourself: Will you tell Jesus you're sorry for your sins? Will you ask Jesus to forgive you, be your personal savior, and take you to heaven when you die?"
- "Let's talk to Jesus together. I'll pray first and you can pray after me if you want."
- "Now you belong to Jesus! He has washed away all your sins and He lives in your heart. You will live in heaven with Him forever."
- "Ask Jesus to be king of your life every day. Commit to do what He wants. Try to serve Him at home and school. He is always with you to help you and love you."

Sixth Step. Encourage and Train Them to Love and Serve the Lord

Ultimately, the goal of the Father for your children is not only that they come to know Christ as their Savior, not only that they know and believe His mighty works, not only that they know and obey His inspired Word, but that they choose of their own free will to love and serve Him.

Have you noticed how much this sense of God's calling in our families has gotten lost? We've traded it in for what I sometimes call "Christian appearances"—well-scrubbed, high achieving, perfectly mannered children who wouldn't think of embarrassing their parents with irresponsible social choices, yet who remain nearly inaccessible for God's use.

We seem to have forgotten that our children have been loaned to us as a gift from the Lord, that our purpose is not to use Christianity to give them a safe and secure life but to spend our opportunity as parents to raise them up as godly, committed, and wholly usable servants for God's greater purposes.

This is a critical dividing line between First and Second Chair parents. For the Second Chair mom or dad, church is the best opportunity for their kids to get ahead, to turn out commendably. But the First Chair parent realizes all along that the Lord calls all of his children—our kids included—to a specific life work. The separation between career and ministry almost disappears. Our children are shining lights, wherever they are—and that is why they are there! At every turn, the vocational question comes back to, "What do you think the Lord wants you to do with your life?"

I used to spend a lot of time on Christian college campuses. One of the saddest discoveries I made was how few Christian college students have any kind of understanding or even belief that the Lord has a specific call upon their lives. When I'd ask, "What is your major, and why did you select it?" the majority of answers focused on money, opportunity, or confusion—"I don't know, I kind of like it."

The Bible is clear—we are to be responsible, hard-working men and women of high integrity who produce significant results from our labors. What the Bible is also clear about is that our job is never the supplier of our needs; the Lord is. When decisions are made solely upon the "need to make a living" rather than struggling through the process of "how can I serve the Lord and His Kingdom the most" then you often end up with a life bound by debt, cluttered by insignificant activities, and on a collision course with regret.

Seventh Step. Take the Long View

Parenting doesn't end when your child has left home physically. The Lord didn't call us to parent our children until they turn eighteen. The Lord calls us to a commitment of a lifetime—our contribution to and influence over our children is lifelong. A little time spent in the Book of Proverbs will show you that the counsel of elders—especially elderly parents—is a distilled, priceless, and ongoing source of teaching for the next generation.

Unless you can embrace the lifelong parenting role that the Bible envisions, you are going to experience frequent frustration, disappointment, and even disillusionment. When your children leave or marry, your parenting hasn't ended. A new chapter has started. Their independence from you is a requirement for health and adulthood but their need for you shouldn't diminish so much as change.

You now become a prized mentor and friend. As one of our good friends loves to say, "You move from telling them what to do to asking them what they think they should do." But the parenting influence in that kind of question remains enormous.

I'll never forget one Sunday afternoon when our son Dave called me up for some advice. He was newly married and I could tell he wasn't sure he should still be calling for help. "I guess I ought to figure this out on my own now, right?" he said.

I laughed. "Son, I just got off the phone with my dad. I still need his wisdom so much." I reminded Dave that while all his decisions were now his full responsibility, he didn't ever have to carry the weight of them alone. His mom and I would always be ready to help him think through his options.

My seminary professor, Howard Hendricks, used to say, "You only know the quality of your parenting when you see what your grandchildren become." Ultimately, the Bible threads together not only the parenting relationship between you and your children, but between you and your grandchildren.

I'll admit that in today's hectic world, where our children can move thousands of miles away, it takes more determination to fulfill this important role of parenting past "eighteen and free." Many mornings I pray for our grandchildren by name and ask that the Lord would show me how to be the grandfather to them He wants me to be. As life moves on, most grandparents have more time to invest with their children and grandchildren—and values can be nurtured over the long term.

As you think of your children and grandchildren and your involvement and role with them, is the strand of godliness growing stronger or weaker in the next generations?

Remember Doc Renno?

Despite his age, Doc says he's not about to stop doing what he loves. "No true fiddle maker has the right to lay down his tools," he says. He's quick to remind you that Antonio Stradivari, who made some pretty good fiddles himself three hundred years ago, didn't get to put his now-legendary name on an instrument until he had apprenticed for more than twenty years.

Do you see it now? From the birth of your child onward, you as a parent are a craftsman for God. In your hands is the soul of the next generation, and with every loving master stroke, you are calling it into being for God's glory.

> *You as a parent are a craftsman for God.*

THE LAND OF CONFIDENCE

As you complete this chapter, you may be both encouraged and discouraged. Encouraged because of the things you as a parent have been doing "right," and not as encouraged because of other things you perhaps should be doing. Whatever you do, however, don't be defeated by the past.

The past can't be changed, but the present is God's workshop for making masterpieces anyway. At our fingertips, we always hold the opportunity to set a new direction, to make changes, and to follow through. And He is ready to work through every moment.

Darlene and I both deeply desire to produce in our children exactly what the Lord seeks: godly offspring. This doesn't automatically make us perfect parents. But we don't have to live in a swamp of regret about the past or in those hazy hills of blind hope. Instead, we can live at peace in the clear land of deep confidence. Why? As we parent according to the Lord's revealed methods, we can count on His blessing.

It's really remarkable, isn't it, that the Lord permits us to be personally and deeply involved in His agenda for shaping human beings?

When Doc Renno works over a premium piece of spruce or mahogany, carving, sanding, and finishing, his every effort is intended to bring forth a masterpiece that is ready to vibrate with life. Think of how much more valuable are your efforts as a parent. Rest assured that as you do your part—shaping your children with the truth of God's Word, smoothing away rough corners with His love—your child will indeed become a beautiful, priceless instrument in the Master's hands.

And as you follow these steps to raising godly children, you can rely like a skilled craftsman on the shaping principle of Proverbs 22:6:

> Train up a child in the way he should go,
> And when he is old he will not depart from it.

Chapter Twelve

The Hidden Wound
of Children

BREAKING THROUGH TO FORGIVENESS AND HEALING

*E*ver drive so far over the horizon that you come to the end of
the pavement, then to the end of the road, and then—miles
later in the middle of nowhere—to the end of the jeep track
and the bottom of your gas tank?

I know parents who have that experience with their kids. These
moms and dads may not have left the city limits for years, but in a failed,
frustrated relationship with a child, they have long ago arrived at the back
of beyond. Nothing seems to work anymore. There's nowhere left to go
and no way to get there.

If you know what I'm talking about, this chapter's for you.

Not too long ago, I was coleading a father/son retreat with my son,
David. The conference was jammed with men and boys of all ages. My
son and I were well prepared and excited about the opportunity to
minister together.

The first session Friday night went well, but something seemed to be
missing, and I couldn't put my finger on it. David and I prayed about it
together, then the next morning we set about getting feedback. Of course,
men don't talk much before breakfast, so the interviews ran short.
"Good," "Great," or "Fine" seemed to be the recurring answers. Maybe, we
thought, we were concerned about nothing.

Saturday morning started out well, with all those rows of plaid shirts and baseball caps seeming to be both awake and interested. Still…we wanted more.

This time when David and I met to compare notes, he agreed with me. Something wasn't going right. So we reevaluated our teaching plan. Then we prayed, and wondered, and waited.

By that evening, we both sensed that the Lord wanted us to depart from our plan. When it was time to preach, I stood up and said, "I believe that the Lord has a different agenda this evening. I'm not released to preach the message that I've prepared. But I'm not sure what the Lord has in mind."

At that, I stepped away from the podium and stood in front of the rows of fathers and sons, searching across the auditorium for a clue. I'll tell you, nobody was dozing off right then. In fact, most of the guys had that deer-caught-in-the-headlights look.

Moments passed. Finally, I said, "One of you men must have a major problem that you wish you could solve tonight. If you would be willing to open up and let me help you in front of everyone, then please join me up here."

I took two chairs from the front row of the auditorium and placed them facing each other on the front of the platform.

Still nothing.

"If you are that person," I said, "then you know who you are. If you really want help, raise your hand."

At that instant, a red-bearded man sitting near the front shot up his hand and nearly yelled, "It's me!"

"Are you willing to let me help you in front of all these men?" I asked.

He nodded and started up to the platform. His name was Mike.

I faced his chair toward the audience and mine facing him with my back to the audience. "What's the matter?" I asked.

"I'm angry all the time," he said.

"What are you angry at?"

"I don't know, but I'm angry."

Gently, I probed further. "Mike, have you ever been abusive in your anger?"

"How did you know?" Mike asked, surprised. "Well, sometimes. That's my problem—my anger and my abusive personality."

"That's not your problem," I said, "that's only the external demonstration of a deeper problem. Do you know what it is?"

Silence. Then he shook his head. He had no idea.

"Who has hurt you the most in your life?" I asked.

His response was immediate. "My father. My father never told me that he loved me. Not once in my entire life!"

As those words rushed out, I noticed that Mike broke eye contact with me and looked at the audience. I continued. "Did that hurt you very much?"

"Hurt me? Are you kidding?" His eyes left mine again. He looked over my right shoulder toward the same place in the auditorium as before. "Not once in my entire life...my father...never told me he loved me." As he forced out each word, Mike ground his jaws and pumped the muscles in his forearms.

But he kept looking away. Suddenly it dawned on me that he was actually speaking to someone in the audience. Slowly I turned, following the distraught man's gaze. Right next to Mike's now empty chair sat a distinguished white-haired gentleman who looked even more tense and distraught than Mike.

"My father never told me that he loved me. Not once in my entire life!"

"Sir," I said to him, "are you Mike's father?"

By this time, the rows of men had frozen up completely. They might as well have been chiseled out of granite. No one breathed, no one looked away, because no one including me could believe what was happening right before our eyes.

The white-haired man stood up. "Yes, I am his father," he said.…

That night I stumbled onto a breakthrough of my own. I discovered that a massive number of Christian family members are locked in chains of unforgiveness, bitterness, hatred, and vengeance. The Lord showed me—showed all of us in the room that night—how this injury between a child and a parent keeps family relationships in the dungeon and puts a halt to spiritual maturity.

If you sense a need for help and healing in this area, my heart and my prayers are with you. What you probably feel is exhausted, frustrated, and defeated in your parent-child relationships—at the end of that jeep track with an empty tank!

But God has brought you to this page for a very promising reason, and I believe with His help you'll find it. With Him, you'll experience a spiritual breakthrough in your family that you'll never forget.

I want to return to Mike and his dad, and tell you the rest of that evening's amazing story. But first, let's explore how to identify and break those chains.

THE TRUTH ABOUT SOUL WOUNDS

The more I've examined the emotional injuries that sabotage relationships between parents and children, the more sure I am of several key issues:

- injured relationships account for the overwhelming majority of long-term parenting problems in Christian families;
- when biblical guidelines for raising godly children have been applied and don't seem to be working, injured relationships are usually the culprit; and

- injured relationships are the major, hidden force that drive our children away from First Chair living, and sometimes from the faith altogether.

It's important for us to think through these statements in the context of this book about spiritual breakthroughs. Taken together, these conclusions indicate that the root of an apparent, highly resistant spiritual problem may be a hidden, deeply rooted emotional one.

My term for this incapacitating injury in the heart of a family is "soul wound." Soul wounds are injuries that the eyes can't see, the mind can't seem to explain, but that the heart feels nevertheless. They cause a destructive unraveling in the core of your child's being that affects his or her capacity for healthy relationships with others, especially parents and future spouses, and with God.

To understand how a soul wound might be affecting your child, consider what happens when you sustain a wound, let's say a deep cut to your arm. You become very protective of that arm. Get bumped in an elevator on your new stitches, and you wince and back hastily towards the corner. Get intentionally struck, and you're likely to get angry. And if another person, situation, or object is responsible for that wound, you'll avoid that source at whatever cost.

The same responses apply to emotional and spiritual wounds. If your child has received a heart wound from you or his other parent (or both), he will intuitively put up dividing walls, remaining aloof regardless

The root of an apparent, highly resistant spiritual problem may be a hidden, deeply rooted emotional one.

of what you say or do. Why? Because he's seeking the safety of distance rather than the risk of intimacy. He may express sudden anger or overreact in a variety of ways. He may spiral into self-destructive behavior.

But there's a key difference. Soul wounds are often hidden, like camouflaged enemy soldiers, from both parent and child.

Imagine the parents' frustration in the following scenarios if, as is often the case, they have no idea that a wound exists, much less that they are its cause:

- They move affectionately and innocently toward a son, and he instinctively backs away behind a veil of excuses or diversions.
- They try to impose sensible limits or discipline on a daughter, but she screams obscenities, and maybe runs away.
- They strive to pass along the legacy of godliness which they hold so dear, but the child stubbornly rejects it, either passively or outright.

A common indication in a child of a hidden soul wound is that the child tries to salve his or her pain in wrong places and with destructive intensity. Unfortunately, a common response from clueless parents is to try to "fix" behaviors rooted in their child's invisible wounds with all sorts of wrong solutions.

Right about now you might be thinking, "I've never cursed at my son, or struck him in anger!" or "But their father and I have stayed together *just for them!*"

I must tell you that the most tenacious wounds are often the most deeply buried ones, the least expected, the most easily dismissed. Do you ever wonder about the impact of your wrong choices on your children? Could they have felt abandoned or neglected by you? Could Second Chair living in your life—compromises, contradictions, lack of integrity—be the cause of painful internal conflicts for your growing child?

Even if you think the answer *might* be a yes, I urge you to count on the fact that your child has a root of unforgiveness, bitterness, anger, hidden hatred, and even vengeance toward you. Your child loves you (God created him or her to love you and need you), but because of the injury, he or she also hates you. You'll get nowhere until you face the wound and deal with it together. And a wonderful spiritual breakthrough is waiting for you when you do.

Remember as you go through this chapter that not only do you have children, but you also are a child. Hidden in your own heart may be a similar wound. If such a wound exists and you are willing to deal with it now, I guarantee that many confusing, frustrating, and hurtful things in your life will soon become clear.

All this talk of injury at the heart of a relationship that matters so much to you can be terribly disheartening to a mom or dad, I know. But there's hope and wholeness ahead. Before this chapter is over, you will know exactly what to do to heal such wounds. You will set yourself and your family free from hidden chains. And once you make this break-through real, others will quickly follow.

HOW SOUL WOUNDS HAPPEN

A soul wound can creep into almost any relationship, even the most well-intentioned. A hard-driving dad makes some false assumptions about what will motivate his son. A mother who wants the best for her daughter is blind to how much her relationship with the girl is affected (even distorted) by unmet needs in her own life. Believers who operate primarily as First Chair parents aren't exempt. Misunderstandings can take root. Areas of our lives may still need spiritual breakthroughs—and our children may be suffering for the lack of them. And after all, we're still human, and humans are continually in need of forgiveness.

Yet I believe that the occasions when a Christ-honoring parent wounds his child intentionally are infrequent. In my experience, most wounding is caused by a parent who is living apart from the Lord to some degree.

Let's just put it in the language of this book: Second Chair parents wound their children far more than First Chair parents. Not, however, because they aren't as nice, don't care as much for their children, or are in any way second-rate people. The problem stems from the kind of commitments they're living by that define the child-raising experience. When you sit in the Second Chair, you live a life of compromise not commitment; of me and God, not God and me; of valuing possessions more than people; of serving yourself and not serving the Lord; of a Christianity based on appearances and responsibility, not on a compelling relationship of the heart.

The consequence of these Second Chair commitments is that a parent will always tend to pursue them *outside* the boundaries of the big hunks of time and energy that the Lord made all children to need from their parents. Taken alone, this, I believe, is the most common source of injury to a child. Conflict occurs between the need of the child for the parent and the need of the parent for personal peace, pleasure, and possessions. Most of the time, parents push their children away without even knowing it. They're so busy making a good life happen under their own steam, they simply miss the danger signs that an observant parent operating with First Chair priorities would tend to pick up.

Conflict occurs between the need of the child for the parent and the need of the parent for personal peace, pleasure, and possessions.

Because the Second Chair parent's heart is still strongly committed to self, the child easily becomes an obstacle or a source of irritation. Every time the parent chooses self over the child, the child gets cut. "Later," "I'm too tired," "Next time, I promise," "Not now, I'm watching the ball game," "Can't you find anything else to do but bother me?" or "I wish I could go to your birthday party, but something came up at work"—each one is a cut to the heart. In the early years, the child seems to adjust. But as time passes and the child matures, a protective callus appears. The child learns to compensate for his losses in unhealthy ways. A soul wound develops.

So why don't caring parents turn things around? Don't they realize what they are doing?

It's my observation that they can't—even when they genuinely try. Why? Because as long as they sit in the Second Chair and remain committed to themselves more than the Lord, all their parenting decisions will be motivated by guilt, polluted with frustration, and diluted by a persistent sense of obligation. To a sensitive child, these attempts to make things right soon become indistinguishable from the problem.

Even when the family does make a turnaround, it seldom lasts. Generally I'd blame this on the fact that guilt is an overrated, underpowered agent for change. Guilt is a strong but temporary negative emotion. Have you noticed? Guilt feelings fade rapidly as familiarity with the problem grows, even with a determination to do something about the problem. But that's before anything *has* actually changed. And once the unwanted feelings are gone, so is the motivation. That's why so many parents who make the right decision but for the wrong reason rarely enjoy the success they intuitively know should be theirs.

The Old Testament's closing prophecy addresses this issue exactly:

Behold, I will send you Elijah the prophet
Before the coming of the great and dreadful day of the Lord.
And he will turn
The hearts of the fathers to the children,
And the hearts of the children to their fathers,
Lest I come a strike the earth with a curse. (Malachi 4:5–6)

Although this is a prophetic passage, you can't miss the need for the heart to "turn" in both directions—parent to child and child to parent. Interestingly, this same prophecy is applied to John the Baptist and further clarifies its meaning for us. When the angel spoke to Zacharias about the birth of his son, John, he described him with these words:

"He [John the Baptist] will also be filled with the Holy Spirit, even from his mother's womb. And he will turn many of the children of Israel to the Lord their God. He will also go before Him [the Messiah] in the spirit and power of Elijah, 'to turn the hearts of the fathers to the children,' and the disobedient to the wisdom of the just to make ready a people prepared for the Lord." (Luke 1:15b-17)

Both of these passages show us that the sin of fathers in turning away from the Lord and to disobedience is directly related to the fathers' turning their hearts away from their children.

Sin toward God produces sin toward one's children. Hardness of heart toward God produces hardness of heart toward one's children. Turning away from God leads to turning away from one's offspring. A broken relationship with the Lord may eventually lead to a broken relationship with your child. The relationship parents have with the Lord is always the root and controlling factor that determines the type of relationship they have with their child.

No wonder Malachi in his exhortation about producing godly offspring states that since God seeks godly offspring from your marriage, you need to take heed to your spirit (Malachi 2:15). And now we can see the common thread of violence to relationships that occurs between us and those we love most if we don't guard our hearts for God.

I sincerely believe that until Christians understand and fully embrace First Chair living, they will always struggle with their role as parent. Until they move into the First Chair, become committed to the Lord above self, and then embrace His goal of raising "godly offspring" as a parent's most important goal, they will forever experience double-mindedness, frustration, and even depression.

Follow me now as together we seek the path of healing in yourself and in your family's soul.

How to Heal Your Children's Soul Wounds

There's an ancient Chinese saying about facing your fears: "Always run toward the dragon." That might sound like cocky advice to you, but every Chinese boy knows what it means. They think of Chinese New Year celebrations, when boys like to dash around trailing dragon kites tied to little sticks. The colorful paper kites stream out behind them, filled like a wind sock at an airport. In parades, teams of men run through the streets holding up giant, blocks-long versions of the same dragon kites. If they keep running, the dragon rides high and huge, filled with air. If they turn and run toward the dragon, it immediately deflates and sinks to the ground, nothing but a pile of paper.

What should you do about the soul wound that may be threatening and defeating your family right now? Don't wait or flee or quibble. Turn around. Go toward the wound, my friend. As you faithfully and prayerfully go toward the source of the pain, what may now seem gigantic, terrifying, and impossible to overcome will start to flutter and flap and fold and sink.

In God's good time, the dragon of pain will be scraps of paper and a memory. Here's a step-by-step process that has helped many parents just like you:

1. Start by Dealing with Your Own Heart Wounds

It is the perfect and complete will of God that you have a deep and meaningful relationship with every one of your children and that through that relationship you train and influence your children to grow and become men and women who heaven characterizes as your godly offspring.

It is also the perfect and complete will of God that you yourself be whole through and through. And in order to heal soul wounds with your own children, you too must find healing for any wounds with your own parents.

When this healing begins, incredible parenting breakthroughs become possible. I remember being intercepted in the parking lot of a church after a day of preaching on this topic. A mother and her sixteen-year-old daughter ran up to me.

"I just had to tell you," the mother said, "that on the way into the service this morning, I told my daughter that I thought it was impossible to ever have a relationship with my mother again. I had no idea what you were going to talk about!"

She looked over to her daughter and then back at me. "As I listened," she said, "I realized that my heart was filled with unforgiveness and hatred for my mother. She was and is completely selfish. Really, she never could give love to me in the way that I needed and deserved. But I also realized today that my bitterness toward my own mother is seeping into my relationship with my own daughter."

She paused as if to gather courage. "And, I knew that my mother would never apologize for what she's done." Tears welled up in her eyes.

"I'm so sorry," I said.

But she continued. "So after the service this morning, I called her up in California. I told her I needed to forgive her and then told her all the ways she had hurt me and that I forgave her for every single wound. I told her I wasn't going to hate her any longer. I said, 'Mom, I forgive you, and I'm giving my heart back to you even if you hurt it again. I'm going to love you anyway!'"

In order to heal soul wounds with your own children, you too must find healing for any wounds with your own parents.

I was touched by her story. "What happened then?" I asked.

"Oh, a long silence," she said. "I thought that the phone must have gone dead. But finally Mother started talking. I still can't believe what she said. It was: 'Sweetheart, I'm so sorry. Please forgive me. My heart hurts for you. Please come and see me!'"

By this time, the teenage daughter had big tears rolling down her cheeks. "We're going to fly out together," the woman said. "The three of us are going to have a good old girls' cry, and then we're going to get started making up for all those lost years."

By God's grace, the healing in this family was going to spread through three generations. You see, once the child in you, the parent, becomes a candidate for healing, the legacy of wounding which you dread can be exchanged for a legacy of love. Your children will inherit blessing from you instead of blight.

2. Admit That You Have Wounded Your Child

Come to grips with the fact that you've wounded your child, either purposefully or accidentally. Don't permit yourself to rationalize, defend yourself, or tell yourself that they probably deserved it. Unless you come to fully believe that you have injured your child and shouldn't have, don't even come close to moving to the next step. Your child will see through you in a second.

3. Prepare Your Heart for the Pain You Will Feel

This is going to be "heart surgery" on both of you—and no matter how much you wished that it wouldn't hurt you or your child, it will. After all, the reason those wounds are still infected is because your child found, for whatever reason, that they were too difficult or painful to deal with. Layers of coping mechanisms have piled up. A flat-out denial that there is a problem may be the first thing from your child's lips—and what you most want to hear—but don't believe it until you have completed the process and God has shown you the whole truth.

Spend time praying through what you have done and how it has or might have affected your child. Ask the Lord for the insight and wisdom He promises. Ask Him to put you in touch with your feelings and create in you a tender empathy and respect for your child's feelings. If you still don't come to the place where you genuinely regret your part in what has happened and desperately turn, your heart isn't ready.

4. Select the Time and Place Carefully

A conversation with an injured child about something as deep as a soul wound is likely to be one of the most difficult conversations of your life. At least at the beginning.

Choose a private place that is comfortable for both of you. Take a walk in a nearby park if physical activity helps you relax. Take a drive in the country if one or both parties might talk more easily with all eyes forward. Or choose a dark corner in a restaurant.

Pick a time when there's nothing limiting the length of your conversation. I recommend after dinner around 8:00 P.M. Seems to me most of us loosen up a bit in the later evening and are more open to talking transparently. Then do your part to get prayed up and emotionally prepared for the task.

In these initiating moments with your child, be particularly careful to read your child's body language and eye contact. Protect his or her feelings of safety as much as possible. The Holy Spirit will help you.

Sometimes the need is so great that you don't look for the best time—you make the time right at that very moment. I remember hanging over a ranch rail out West one hot, dusty day, finding myself deep in conversation with a young wrangler. Even though I'd just met him, I could tell he was lost and discouraged. Before long, I sensed a deep soul wound from his father. And that was the beginning of an incredible chain of events—a reaching for forgiveness, a decision to fly back home to work things out with his parents, and a major turnaround in his whole family. Today he's a happy and stable married man with a promising future. And it all began with a few words shared over a fence. I can still smell the horse stalls and hear the flies buzzing in the heat. But God had made an appointment for both of us, and he will do the same for you and your children.

5. Ask Their Permission to Talk with Them about Something Personal

You have been preparing for hours, days, or even weeks. You gave yourself permission to move down this difficult path. But your child has no idea what is going to happen. Clearly and simply, ask your child if it is okay with them for you to talk about something that is personal to you and may be difficult for them to handle. After you've asked the question, be quiet, don't ramble, and give him or her the opportunity to answer.

If your child says yes, they've opened a little of their heart to you. You can proceed to the next step. Suggest the time and place you have in mind, hopefully at that very moment.

If the answer is no, don't express frustration or try to argue. Never ask why they aren't ready. Respond with an okay and a smile, and tell your child that because this matter is so important to you, you'll put the request to them again sometime in the future. Then, change the subject.

> *Be particularly careful to read your child's body language and eye contact.*

6. Share with Them That You've Realized That You Have Hurt Them

When you're both securely in the conversational spot of your choosing, focus on what your child must be feeling and wondering. Most kids feel threatened, or at least instinctively flinch, when a parent wants to talk introspectively about pain and failure in the parent-child relationship.

Keep this in mind when you introduce your subject: You believe you have hurt your child and may still be hurting him or her; you are deeply sorry about that and you want to change things.

Your admission that you have hurt them may be very surprising. And because your words prick like a lance into their infected wounds, your child may recoil with discomfort. Outwardly, your child will probably react in one of three ways:

- immediate tears and agreement that indeed you have,
- the silent treatment with a look of sullen rebellion, or
- a quick and impetuous denial that any such thing happened or could have happened.

No matter what their reaction, you are the one who must keep talking. Share your heart with them, and how deeply sorry you are that you have injured them.

7. Ask For Their Forgiveness for Every Single Wound You Committed

The infection in your child's heart (regardless of age) can only be lanced and then cleansed by the choice of your child to forgive you for the *specific* wound. If you say, "I'm sorry for hurting you; will you forgive me?" they may, but it won't make much of a difference.

Remember the cleansing steps we took in chapter 5? Wounds are specific, so forgiveness must be specific. Proceed through your conversation with the assumption that you must treat numerous pockets of injury and unforgiveness one at a time.

How does a mom or dad find words for moments like these?

> *No matter what their reaction, you are the one who must keep talking.*
>
>

- Don't cast blame. Don't explain or defend. Don't theorize or preach. And don't come to conclusions or choose feelings for your child.
- Do talk simply and directly, keeping eye contact. Take responsibility for yourself and your parenting role.

- Listen carefully. Listen for God's direction. Listen, not just for your child's words, but for what he or she is struggling to say behind them.

Start with words like, "I realized that I really hurt you when I stayed at work for your seventh birthday, and I'm so sorry. Will you forgive me?" Then wait for your child's answer before proceeding to the next wound.

The first apologies may seem terribly difficult for both you and your child. Be patient. As layers of numbness, scarring, or forgetfulness are peeled away, the oil of forgiveness will start to flow, and your hearts will open more and more to each other.

It's the rare family that doesn't need at least one of these "heart-cleansings" from the years of parenting. Sometimes the wounds are known, but many times, they lay buried beneath layers of emotional scabbing that must ultimately be broken through for the infection to be released.

I remember the day I asked my older daughter, Jennifer, to go for an afternoon drive. I had come to realize that I had wounded her—now it was up to me to invite healing.

How hard it was to get those first few sentences out! How difficult to admit that I had hurt someone I love so dearly. Our conversation lasted more than an hour as we drove 'round and 'round the neighborhood. Injury by injury, I asked for her forgiveness. And with each injury, tears flowed for both of us, but by the time we were back in the driveway, our hearts had started to mend.

Many years have passed since then, and I look back on those as some of the most important miles I ever drove. And how thankful I am that Jenny and I are closer today than I ever dreamed possible. When the hurt is released, the heart can embrace. Thank you, Jenny.

8. When You Can't Think of Any More, Ask Them "What Else?"

Count on it. There's no way you can remember or know every wound. But your child *does* know. The truth as they have lived it is stored away in their bones somewhere, even if it's not on the tip of their tongue. Your job is to help your child open up in every area.

When you're done with your list, say, "I know I've hurt you in other ways. What's one hurt that has really bothered you?"

Regardless of their response, other injuries almost certainly exist. If there's no reply, share your heart so that your child can hear again that you really are repentant and desperately want their forgiveness. Repeat the question. Eventually, other wounds will surface. Remember not to defend yourself. The wound is real in them, period, and only your apology can release them to experience healing.

As you follow these steps, anticipate tears and grief from both of you. That's because the granting of forgiveness is profoundly healing for both giver and receiver.

As your conversation ends, thank your child. Tell them again that you love them. Then ask: "Will you open your heart back up to me and tear down the walls that you've put up to protect yourself?" If your child chooses to open his or her heart to you, tearing down any protective walls, you'll have entered a relationship with your child that you thought was only possible in storybooks.

TERRIBLE BEGINNINGS CAN HAVE WONDERFUL FOREVERS

What happened between Mike and his dad? We left you earlier with Mike staring angrily from the platform, and his father standing white-haired and ashen-faced in the audience.

Leaving Mike on the platform, I walked down the center aisle until I stood near the dad. "Sir, would you like this injury in your life to be healed?"

He nodded.

"Then please come with me," I said, and I walked with him up to the front and sat him in my chair, which was still facing his son. The only thing pounding louder than my heart were my hands pounding on the doors of heaven for immediate guidance, discernment, and spiritual sensitivity. Down deep, however, I knew the Lord was in charge and that He was fully trustworthy.

With both Mike and his dad now up in front, I turned the two chairs so they faced each other, only a couple of feet apart, with their sides toward the audience. I knelt behind the chairs and asked the father, "Sir, is it true that you never told your son in his whole life that you loved him?"

The truth as they have lived it is stored away in their bones somewhere, even if it's not on the tip of their tongue.

Again he nodded, choking with emotion.

Again I asked, "Would you like to change all that right now?"

Again he nodded. Then he leaned toward me and whispered hoarsely, "I never thought this day would come."

"Sir," I said, "place your hands on your son's shoulders and tell him you love him." Up went his arms with his hands resting on his son's broad shoulders. Tears brimmed in Mike's eyes.

The father said, "Son, I love you." But the words sounded hollow, and Mike's body language was yelling, "I don't believe you!" I sensed the men in the auditorium felt the same way.

"Sir, if you were my father and told me that you loved me that way, I don't think I would believe you," I ventured. "Why don't you say those words again. Reach way into your heart."

The father took a deep breath. "Mike…son," he began. He seemed to be hauling unfamiliar words and feelings up from the depths. "I really do love you."

Walls tottered and started to fall. "That was good, friend," I said. "Now I ask you to say those words again from your heart, but this time I want you to say them through your eyes, into his eyes, and right down to his heart."

This time, love poured out of that old, clogged heart as if an ancient dam had burst. Father and son embraced while the roomful of other fathers and sons watched this holy moment.

Then I asked Mike, "Do you believe your father loves you?"

Now it was Mike who could only nod his head, tears streaming down his face and beard.

"Sir," I said back to his father, "would you now please put your hands back on your son's shoulders and bless him? Tell him of your hopes and dreams for him right here—in front of us, your brothers. Express your confidence and affirmation in what God is doing, and will yet do, in his life. Bless your son in Jesus' name. Will you do that as best you can and in your own words?"

> *"Bless your son in Jesus' name. Will you do that as best you can and in your own words?"*

You should have heard the father's blessing. It was absolutely incredible. Dreams long abandoned seemed to find words and spring to life.

When his father was done, I turned to Mike. "Is your heart healed, Mike?" I asked. Then before he could answer, I pressed home. "I mean, Mike, do you think you have a reason to still be angry or abusive?"

That's when it happened. Rows of men and boys witnessed a child's soul scar begin to fade. Mike suddenly understood that his anger wasn't against his wife or children but against his father. And the father could experience freedom from his prison of silence and distance. The hard lines on both their faces softened. Before our eyes, they seemed to change and grow younger. When the men walked off the platform arm-in-arm, the audience stood and gave a thunderous applause.

Yet when we were seated again, I sensed from God that we were not finished. Scanning the faces of the auditorium, I recognized similar pain everywhere. Praying for grace, I plunged ahead. "How many of you have soul wounds from your father that have crippled your life to this point?" I asked.

Nearly every hand went up. I even heard quiet groans from several directions....

That evening as David and I slowly walked back to my hotel room, we thanked the Lord for His grace and mercy. I was thankful for the power of God's Word and His Spirit working in our hearts to break down barriers, to heal families, and to make all things new.

Think about it: The truth of His Word is so powerful, if we just followed exactly what it says, we could—and would—enjoy a breakthrough that could turn our families around for Him.

My friend, do you have a soul wound, or have you given a soul wound, or both?

Take courage. On this path of speaking the truth in love and forgiveness, God has a spiritual breakthrough waiting for you of joy nearly unspeakable!

Multnomah Publishers

The publisher and author would love to hear your comments about this book. *Please contact us at:*
www.thebreakthroughseries.com

Epilogue

I'll always remember the face of that angry reporter. He was a big man with fire in his eyes, and when I walked into the press box at the Silverdome in Detroit, he already had his microphone shoved in my direction.

"You don't mean to tell me, do you, Dr. Wilkinson," he nearly roared, "that all this is going to make any difference tomorrow?"

Behind him, I could see thousands of men still returning to their seats. They were Promise Keepers who had flooded to the front of the stadium in response to the message of this book. On either side of the reporter, other journalists pressed in.

"You don't *really* think," the first reporter continued, "that all these men walking down the aisles to make a decision—all this emotional spectacle, this going up front—is going to change a single thing in the long run, do you?" He paused, daring me to dodge his bullet. The other media present held out their microphones, leaned eagerly in my direction, and waited.

My mind went blank. I blinked. But then as quickly as I could breathe a prayer for help, a response came.

"Sir, thank you for that question," I said. "It's a terrific one. But let me answer with a question of my own. Did you by any chance get married in a church?"

Now it was the reporter's turn to blink. "Well, yes, I did, but…"

"And on that occasion, did you walk down an aisle, and were you a little emotional?"

"Well, yes," he said, looking confused.

"And did you make a decision when you walked down that aisle that changed the rest of your life?"

"Yes, sir, I did."

"Well, I guess if it worked for you, it can work for ten thousand other men, don't you think?"

Everyone in the room laughed, and so did my interrogator.

A choice that can change a life? *Absolutely!*

What that reporter almost missed is that our lives, from one end to the other, are a sum of our commitments. If you could turn around and look back over your life right now, you would see it mapped out by turning points that got you where you are today. You went left instead of right. You said yes instead of no. You left behind dozens of decent options; one, you embraced.

In the same way, your life is the sum total of your spiritual breakthroughs. And I hope by now as you look back over the pages and chapters of this book, you see many. If you do, I know beyond a doubt that each one is already making a difference in your life.

"But now," you might be asking, "what can I do to keep breaking through spiritually a way of life?"

My advice to you is simple, at times costly—and utterly critical. You must keep deciding. Keep walking that aisle. Keep turning away from all that is self and sin and second best—and reach for the radical, blessed choice of First Chair living. Because the choice (and every day offers hundreds) is always up to you.

Think of this choice as a lifestyle of repentance; that is, you acknowledge that without a continual willingness on your part to let go of what you impulsively reach for most naturally, God cannot fill your life with the pure best He longs to give you. A lifestyle of repentance means being quick to apologize to God, quick to make amends, and courageous enough to pick up again where you left off. A lifestyle of repentance means your spiritual breakthroughs will continue to add up, and God's grace and power will flow through your life in greater and greater abundance.

Take hold of this lifestyle of repentance as your greatest breakthrough yet—the one where you become, as the New Testament puts it, "a living sacrifice" (Romans 12:1). Early Christians knew what that term meant because they were very familiar with temple sacrifices. A sacrifice was a dead animal, killed as a religious offering. Not pretty.

But don't miss Paul's inspired coupling of those two words—"living" and "sacrifice." You see, in a very real sense, you only have value to God's kingdom—you only touch the world for Him—between the moment you come to new life in Christ and the moment you enter His presence eternally. During that space of time, however long or short it may be, God asks you to be a living sacrifice for Him—to die to self, to give away all your personal rights, to cut all the strings, to simply trust Him with all your needs and hopes and dreams completely.

That is the breakthrough lifestyle God is now offering to you—for your best and for His glory.

A living sacrifice.

Choosing to turn, and turn again.

Friend, let's keep walking that aisle joyfully and expectantly together.

I beseech you therefore, brethren, by the mercies of God, that you present your bodies a living sacrifice, holy, acceptable to God, which is your reasonable service.

And do not be conformed to this world, but be transformed by the renewing of your mind, that you may prove what is that good and acceptable and perfect will of God. (Romans 12:1–2)

RESOURCES

Experiencing Spiritual Breakthroughs is a joint project of three Christian organizations who joined together to develop this ministry tool for you. LifeWay Resources (800-233-1123, www.lifeway.com), Multnomah Publishers (800-929-0910, www.multnomahpubl.com), and Walk Thru the Bible (800-868-9300, www.walkthru.org) each brought their strengths to produce the following ministry tools:

1. Video Series

A four-part video series of Dr. Bruce Wilkinson presenting *Experiencing Spiritual Breakthroughs* with compelling dramas and graphics, available for Sunday schools, home Bible studies, evening church services, camps, and conferences. A course workbook and leaders' guide accompanies the series. Available from LifeWay Resources and Walk Thru the Bible.

2. Audio Series

Four audio tapes containing the sound track of each of Dr. Wilkinson's four sessions of the *Experiencing Spiritual Breakthroughs* course on one side with specially prepared daily devotionals and life-changing insights on the second side. Available from LifeWay Resources and Walk Thru the Bible.

3. 30 Days to Experiencing Spiritual Breakthroughs

This book collects thirty of the best articles on how to break through in your life, your marriage, your family, and the Lord. Written by such authors such as James Dobson, Oswald Sanders, Andrew Murray, Charles Swindoll, Gary Smalley, and Joseph Stowell. Can be used separately or read in conjunction with the course. Available from Multnomah and Walk Thru the Bible.

4. Experiencing Spiritual Breakthroughs Conferences

Special conferences for churches, colleges, conference centers, and camps on the life-changing principles of the Three Chairs. Call Walk Thru the Bible for details.

More Insightful Books

by Dr. Bruce Wilkinson

The Seven Laws of the Learner
Written for teachers, parents, and professionals, this scriptural book outlines principles and techniques that revolutionize the ability to teach for life change.
ISBN 0-88070-464-0

Almost Every Answer for Practically Any Teacher!
This book contains one hundred articles that provide insight, inspiration, and instruction for those who communicate God's truth at school, church, home, or in the workplace.
ISBN 0-88070-473-X

30 Days to Experiencing Spiritual Breakthroughs
This tool for spiritual growth presents thirty practical articles that show readers how to experience breakthroughs in their Christian lives, marriages, families, and walks with God.
ISBN 1-57673-982-1

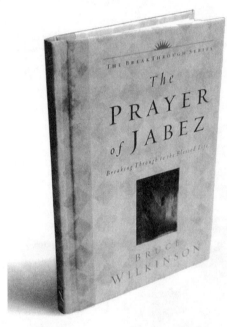

Maximize Your Impact for God with the
BreakThrough Series Book Two, *Secrets of the Vine.*™

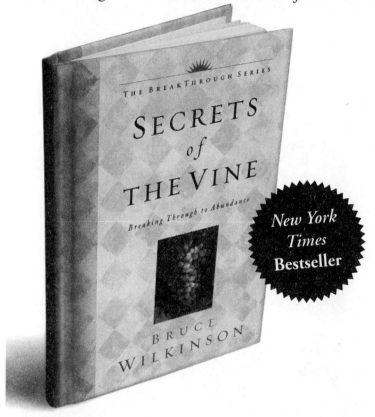

Dr. Bruce Wilkinson explores John 15 to show readers how to make
maximum impact for God. Dr. Wilkinson demonstrates how Jesus
is the Vine of life, discusses four levels of "fruit bearing" (doing the
good work of God), and reveals three life-changing truths that will
lead readers to new joy and effectiveness in His kingdom.

ISBN 1-57673-975-9

Also available on audiocassette: ISBN 1-57673-977-5
Audio CD: ISBN 1-57673-908-2

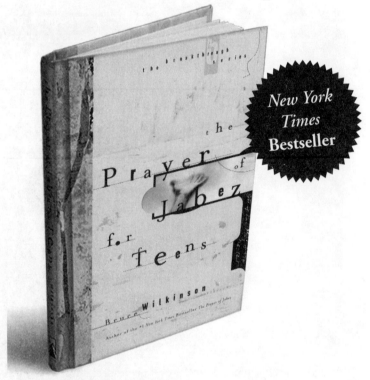

You've Heard What the World Says about Marriage.

But What Does the Word Say?

Introducing A Biblical Portrait of Marriage Video Series.

Who better to strengthen your marriage than the One who invented it in the first place? Here, at last, is practical, life-changing advice drawn directly from the pages of God's Word.

IN-LAWS OR OUT-LAWS? (#53870) reveals how to turn a potentially negative relationship into a real asset. BALANCE SHEET FOR MARRIAGE (#53880) teaches how the "discipline of contentment" can restore order to your finances. THE BEAUTY OF INTIMATE LOVE (#53890) will help return passion to your marriage by applying biblical principles for sexuality. KEEP THE HEART FIRES BURNING (#53900) shares how to make romance a permanent part of married life. SPEAKING THE TRUTH IN LOVE (#53910) explores how to undo the damage from years of poor communication. And last but certainly not least, FOR BETTER, FOR WORSE—FOREVER (#53920) shows you how to avoid those small, day-to-day disloyalties that undermine your marriage over the long term.

Each of the six forty-minute videos opens and closes with a compelling drama about a family tackling real-life problems. But the heart of the video is the inspiring, biblically based teaching of Dr. Bruce Wilkinson, founder of Walk Thru the Bible ministries.

A Biblical Portrait of Marriage videos are perfect for personal use or church use. To order any one title for just $19.99 or the complete set of six for $99.00 (#53940), call Walk Thru the Bible at 1-800-763-5433.